WISHES
WON'T BRING
RICHES

WISHES WON'T BRING RICHES

NAPOLEON HILL

A TarcherPerigee Book

tarcherperigee

An imprint of Penguin Random House LLC
375 Hudson Street
New York, New York 10014

Copyright © 2018 by The Napoleon Hill Foundation

TarcherPerigee with tp colophon is a registered trademark of
Penguin Random House LLC.

MENTAL DYNAMITE is a registered trademark of The Napoleon Hill Foundation.

Most TarcherPerigee books are available at special quantity discounts for
bulk purchase for sales promotions, premiums, fund-raising, and educational needs.
Special books or book excerpts also can be created to fit specific needs.
For details, write: SpecialMarkets@penguinrandomhouse.com.

Library of Congress Cataloging-in-Publication Data

Names: Hill, Napoleon, 1883–1970, author.
Title: Wishes won't bring riches / Napoleon Hill.
Description: New York : TarcherPerigee, 2018. |
Series: The mental dynamite series |
Identifiers: LCCN 2018002831 (print) | LCCN 2018015763 (ebook) |
ISBN 9781101992852 (ebook) | ISBN 9780143111542 (paperback)
Subjects: LCSH: Self-actualization (Psychology) | Motivation (Psychology) |
BISAC: SELF-HELP / Motivational & Inspirational. | SELF-HELP / Personal
Growth / Success. | BUSINESS & ECONOMICS / Motivational.
Classification: LCC BF637.S4 (ebook) | LCC BF637.S4 H5455 2018 (print) |
DDC 158.1—dc23
LC record available at https://lccn.loc.gov/2018002831

Printed in the United States of America
1 3 5 7 9 10 8 6 4 2

Book design by Elke Sigal

CONTENTS

✳

YOUR "OTHER SELF"
COMES TO YOUR AID
ONLY THROUGH
THE POWER OF
YOUR FAITH.

FOREWORD

By *Don M. Green,*
Executive Director, the Napoleon Hill Foundation

Napoleon Hill wrote seventeen booklets in 1941, each one explaining one of the principles of success he had first learned
from Andrew Carnegie when he interviewed him in 1908. Napoleon was a young magazine reporter at the time, assigned to interview Mr. Carnegie, and Mr. Carnegie was so impressed with him
that he commissioned him to research and write a philosophy of personal achievement. Napoleon spent the next twenty years meeting
with successful men and he wrote what he learned in the classic 1928
book *Law of Success.* In 1937 he wrote a condensed version, which he
titled *Think and Grow Rich.*

The 1941 booklets were titled *Mental Dynamite,* which was a
phrase used by Andrew Carnegie to describe the seventeen principles of success. Each booklet contained lengthy excerpts from Napoleon's interview with Mr. Carnegie, and an analysis of the featured
principle by Napoleon. Within months of their publication, the
United States entered World War Two, and the booklets were set

aside by an understandably preoccupied nation. The Napoleon Hill Foundation has now retrieved them from its archives and is publishing them for a new generation of readers.

In this book, the foundation has assembled three of Dr. Hill's booklets explaining how actions can be used to achieve objectives once a Definite Major Purpose has been selected and a plan conceived to achieve it. These chapters therefore begin once the thought process has been successfully concluded. As Napoleon states in chapter 3, "Plan your work, and work your plan." This book starts after the plan has been made, and concentrates on how to work it.

In chapter 1, "Applied Faith," Napoleon begins by setting forth that portion of his 1908 interview with Andrew Carnegie focusing on this principle. Mr. Carnegie tells young Napoleon that he needs Applied Faith in order to carry out his twenty-year assignment of preparing a philosophy of success. He explains the differences between blind faith, passive faith, and active faith. Mr. Carnegie identifies the capabilities of the mind in an almost poetic fashion, then explains to Napoleon that these capabilities cannot be obtained until fears and self-imposed limitations are replaced by Applied Faith. Action, persistence, and repetition are required to develop such faith, and once it is developed it permits Infinite Intelligence to take control and achieve the objects of one's plans.

After recounting his interview with Mr. Carnegie, Dr. Hill provides two personal stories illustrating how he has used Applied Faith to achieve success. The first recounts that he lost all his money when the banks failed during the Great Depression, but he came to understand that the workings of nature and Infinite Intelligence were more important than money, and this discovery produced in him the Applied Faith he needed to persevere. The second recounts the amazing story of his son Blair, born without ears, who, thanks to the

Applied Faith of Napoleon, gained the ability to hear in the absence of any of the physical instruments of hearing.

Dr. Hill then discusses the importance of the ego in attaining success, and points out how it must be controlled. As Mr. Carnegie had said, fear and doubt must be replaced with faith for the ego to attain its desires. Dr. Hill provides examples of men who controlled their own egos, and of men whose egos were controlled by their wives, but in all cases this control was essential to their success. Dr. Hill sums up the importance of Applied Faith by stating that it is "the most powerful law of nature" because it permits one to acquire the physical counterpart of one's desires.

Chapter 2, "Enthusiasm," also begins with excerpts from Napoleon's interview with Andrew Carnegie in 1908. Mr. Carnegie states that enthusiasm is necessary to clear the mind of negative elements so that faith may take their place. It is an expression of hope, which is needed to develop faith, and hope, faith, and enthusiasm are all essential to attaining success. Mr. Carnegie details the many impediments to developing and maintaining enthusiasm, such as poor health and use of alcohol or narcotics. He explains how young Napoleon's upbringing in poverty carried with it the seed of an equivalent benefit, namely, the enthusiasm that Napoleon's stepmother instilled in him, which motivated him to become a magazine reporter.

Mr. Carnegie speaks about how enthusiasm, as well as lack thereof, is contagious and can spread throughout a business, institution, or family. It is equivalent to a positive mental attitude, but it must be controlled by self-discipline or it can be misdirected. Every Master Mind alliance must have members who are enthusiastic, but also at least one who is not, to balance out and control the enthusiasm.

In the final analysis, enthusiasm, just like Applied Faith, is necessary to move beyond the thinking phase and act to carry out one's major plan based on a Definite Major Purpose.

Following his presentation of his interview of Mr. Carnegie, Dr. Hill elaborates on what he learned. He states that enthusiasm is "faith in action" and "the action factor of thought," and that it can change a negative attitude to a positive one. He explains how a balanced and harmonious mind is needed to develop enthusiasm. He lists many of the positive things that enthusiasm can accomplish, most importantly converting positive emotions to negative ones and preparing the mind for the development of faith.

Dr. Hill emphasizes the importance of being an effective speaker, because speech is the principal way one exhibits enthusiasm. He then sets forth a long interview he had with inventor Thomas Edison, demonstrating how Mr. Edison's enthusiasm for his work drove him to discover the talking machine and electric lightbulb. Dr. Hill also provides a helpful list of the steps one needs to take to develop enthusiasm. He concludes the chapter with a hopeful look at the future of America and the world, based in major part on his belief that enthusiasm will prevail.

The third "action chapter" selected by our foundation is the principle Dr. Hill refers to as Organized Individual Endeavor. It, too, begins with excerpts from the Andrew Carnegie interview. Mr. Carnegie describes thirty-one characteristics of leadership, and emphasizes the need to take action quickly and not procrastinate. Organized Individual Endeavor requires a purpose, a plan, continuous action, and persistence. A strong desire to achieve is more important than book learning. One need not be a genius to succeed. Mr. Carnegie concludes the interview by telling Napoleon that Napoleon, and the world, will gain material wealth but also spiritual understanding from Napoleon's writing of the philosophy of personal achievement. Material wealth alone is destructive of character, and must be accompanied by spiritual growth and enlightenment.

Dr. Hill follows the interview excerpts with an analysis of Organized Individual Endeavor. Only two percent of the people succeed, and this is due to one or more of forty human faults that are the enemies of Organized Individual Endeavor. He lists a number of successful men who followed this principle, and states that it is the "master of defeatism." He tells the story of two men who succeeded by using Organized Individual Endeavor. One was well educated, the other was not, but they both exploited the strengths they possessed. Dr. Hill emphasizes the importance of taking inventory of one's strengths, then using them to achieve one's goals. He states that you need to "plan your work, and work your plan."

The three principles explained in this book teach you how to convert your plans into action. Thinking, hoping, and dreaming are not enough—you must act to achieve your goals. As Napoleon Hill states, "Wishes won't bring riches."

INTRODUCTION TO CHAPTER ONE

B ecause of the profoundness of the subject of this chapter it seems appropriate to approach it with a prepared mind; therefore I take the liberty of offering this brief introductory analysis of Applied Faith.

First, let us take notice of the word "applied."

The purpose of the author in using this word is to draw a clear line of distinction between the word Faith, as it is generally interpreted, and the words Applied Faith, as interpreted in this chapter. Most people use the word "Faith" carelessly, and many misuse it where the word "confidence" would more nearly describe their meaning. Many others speak of Faith without any attempt to apply it in connection with their aims and purposes.

The purpose of this chapter is that of describing the exact meaning of Faith, with suggestions for its application in the solution of the daily problems of modern life. The chapter deals with the active, motivating Faith that is put into daily practice, not the theory, of passive Faith.

There is a definite and dependable method by which that state of mind called Faith can be attained. The burden of this chapter is to describe this method, in terms that are clear and understandable. The chapter does not approach the subject of Faith from the viewpoint of theology, this field being left entirely to men who have prepared themselves for it. This explanation is offered to forestall the conclusion, on the part of any student of this philosophy, that this or any other chapter of this book is intended to influence anyone's religious belief.

The only religion with which this philosophy is intended to deal is the broad, general religion of *right thinking* and *right living* in connection with the important problems of human relationship, in the practical affairs of life.

Let me emphasize, here and now, the fact that I have no misconception as to the final source of Faith, regardless of any specific application of this power I may suggest. While it may be largely superfluous of me to describe my conception of the source of Faith, I nevertheless take the liberty of saying that it is my belief that no one may ever reach the state of mind we call Faith without a definite belief in a Supreme Creator. Whenever I use the term Infinite Intelligence, let it clearly be understood, therefore, that I have reference to that Universal Power through which the Creator gives life to every living thing, from the smallest blade of grass to His greatest handiwork, man.

My conception of the term Infinite Intelligence is this: It is the extended shadow, so to speak, of the Divine Creator. The term, as it is used throughout this chapter, has reference to that portion of the Divine Mind which we can recognize and understand as it is manifested through all natural laws by which all manner of life on earth is controlled. Here I am dealing only with such forces and tangible realities as can be explained in connection with the practical problems of life, and it is my purpose to make no claims which are not based solidly upon the known experiences of men who have achieved noteworthy success through the application of this philosophy.

It is my hope that no reader will undertake to assign meanings to my words which I have not intended.

The subject of this chapter is one that should interest the whole of civilization at this time, because it is the consensus of opinion among men who have given long and serious thought to the subject of Faith that the present world crisis has its roots definitely in the wanton disregard for the power of Faith which is so evident everywhere. It is their belief, also, that there is nothing wrong with the world, or with any physical normal individual now living, which cannot be improved or corrected outright through the power of Faith.

In the presentation of this chapter I have not been contented by merely admonishing the readers to have Faith. The world has been doing this ever since the dawn of civilization, but few have made any helpful attempt to describe how one may acquire Faith for the solution of the practical problems of daily life. It is the burden of this chapter to be the exception to this rule by describing and using Faith. Every reader of this philosophy must use his own mind and reach his own conclusions on this profound subject. If this chapter does no more than inspire serious meditation and thought on the subject of Faith, it will have rendered a priceless service, because Faith is a state of mind which can be attained only through earnest self-examination through which the individual comes into a better understanding of the inner workings of his own mind.

Each individual's mind differs from all others. Every person's reaction to the experiences of life is different from that of all others; therefore, the exact process by which any individual clears his mind of negative thoughts and thus prepares it for the inflow of Infinite Intelligence, through the medium of Faith, is something that can best be determined by the individual himself. This is one thing which no person can guide another in accomplishing. I can, however, offer the suggestion that the approach to the development of that state of mind known as Faith can be greatly facilitated by the stimulating influence of Definiteness of Purpose, backed by enthusiasm and desire which have been fanned into a flame of obsession!

Observe, as you read this chapter, the strong emphasis which Andrew Carnegie has given the subject of Definiteness of Purpose backed by action. No desire can become and remain intense without action back of it.

米

APPLIED FAITH

With this chapter I approach a subject which Andrew Carnegie described as "the dynamo of the entire philosophy." By this he meant that Applied Faith is the power that gives to those who use it an effective way to put the Philosophy of American Achievement into action.

In this chapter Mr. Carnegie begins his analysis of Applied Faith by describing its application in the development of self-reliance without which quality no one would benefit greatly by the other chapters of this book.

As far back as the records of civilization are available, there is evidence that the philosophers, the psychologists, and the scientists have recognized the existence of a power, available to mankind, known as Faith, and the history of civilization is replete with evidence that Faith is an irresistible power; that it enables those who use it to rise above seemingly insurmountable obstacles.

Faith is the foundation, the very central core, of every great religion, and despite the fact that it is the most talked-about subject in the entire field of religion, it is unquestionably the least understood of all religious subjects.

Back through the ages mankind has been admonished to "have faith," but I am without access to any authentic record of a satisfactory explanation as to how that state of mind known as Faith can be inspired.

Through this chapter Mr. Carnegie and I will present our views on ways and means of developing Faith, accompanied by reliable evidence of the soundness of our conclusions. The analysis of the subject of Faith here presented will include both the personal experience of the author and a description of my observations of others, in the application of Faith as a usable force in the solution of the individual problems of life.

The analysis will draw attention to the difference between "faith" and "confidence." It will include a definite, workable formula through which that form of confidence known as self-confidence can be vitalized with the greater power of Faith, and thus made irresistible.

In his description of his own method of applying Faith, Andrew Carnegie reveals, for the first time as far as is known, the secret of his astounding achievements; and in so doing he offers every reader a dependable approach to the understanding and use of the power of Faith.

Obviously, no form of application of Faith is as helpful to an individual as that which aids in the development of self-reliance, for it is no mere expression of poetic words when we say, "That which man can believe, man can achieve." There is a certain state of mind which, as all who have experienced it know, serves to inspire one with enthusiasm, initiative, imagination, and Definiteness of Purpose to rise above ordinary difficulties and carry his plans through to success without effective opposition. We refer to this state of mind as self-reliance, but if we examine carefully those occasions on which it serves best, we will discover that it has a quality far superior to mere confidence in self.

The chapter begins with an analysis of self-confidence, precisely as Andrew Carnegie explained his understanding of this subject to his student, Napoleon Hill, upon our meeting in Mr. Carnegie's study in 1908.

HILL:

> Mr. Carnegie, you have inspired me to undertake a job that may require the better portion of my life. The task is one that calls for self-confidence far greater than I possess; therefore I want you to tell me how I can develop the Faith necessary to carry me over the obstacles with which I will likely meet during my research.

CARNEGIE:

> You have asked me a question that should be of keen interest to every person who aims at achievement above mediocrity, and my answer will describe perhaps the most important of the seventeen principles of achievement. You may put it down as Applied Faith, and you should emphasize it as one factor of human achievement which gives power to all who apply it. It is the great equalizing force which truly makes all men equal.

HILL:

> Am I to understand you to say, Mr. Carnegie, that all men are born equal? Do you mean that men who have great self-reliance are born with that trait?

CARNEGIE:

Now let me get you straightened out on this vital point before you make the same mistake that so many others have made, by assuming that individuals who achieve outstanding success are born with some peculiar quality of genius not possessed by others. Self-confidence is a state of mind that is under the control of the individual, and it is not an inborn trait possessed by some and lacking in others. There are varying degrees of self-confidence, the reason for which I will explain later. Supreme self-confidence is based upon Faith in Infinite Intelligence and you may be certain that no one ever attains this state of mind without having first established contact with and a definite belief in Infinite Intelligence.

The starting point in the development of self-confidence is Definiteness of Purpose. That is why this principle is given first place in the philosophy of individual achievement by me and many others.

It is a well-known fact that the man who knows exactly what he wants, has a definite plan for getting it, and is actually engaged in carrying out that plan, has no difficulty in believing his ability to succeed. It is equally well known that the man of indecision, the fellow who flounders around and procrastinates, soon loses confidence in his own ability and winds up doing nothing. There is nothing difficult to understand about this.

HILL:

But what happens when one knows what he wants, has a plan for getting it, puts his plan into operation, and meets with failure? Doesn't failure destroy self-confidence?

CARNEGIE:

Now that is the very question I hoped you would ask. It gives me an opportunity to set you right on a common mistake that many people make. Failure has one peculiar benefit that is deserving of emphasis, and it is the fact that every failure carries with it, in the circumstance of the failure itself, the seed of an equivalent advantage. Examine the records of the truly great leaders in all walks of life and you will discover that their success is in exact proportion to their mastery of failures.

Life has a way of developing strength and wisdom in individuals, through temporary defeat and failure, and do not overlook the fact that there is no such reality as a permanent failure until an experience has been accepted as such.

The power of the mind is so great that it has no limitations other than those which individuals set up in their own minds. The power that removes all limitations from the mind is Faith; and the source of all Faith is belief in Infinite Intelligence. Once you understand this truth you will not need to worry about self-confidence, for you will possess it in abundance. Every great philosopher has reminded us of this truth.

HILL:

But, Mr. Carnegie, most people are not experienced philosophers, and they are not going to believe that every failure carries with it the seed of an equivalent advantage when failure overtakes them, as it must overtake everyone at one time or another. Now, what I want to know is this: What is one going to do when he meets with failure and the experience destroys his confidence in himself? To whom does such a person turn for aid in the restoration of confidence in himself?

CARNEGIE:

You have propounded what may, at first, appear to be a question that is very difficult to answer, but the appearance is deceiving, as I shall explain. Let me answer you briefly in this way: The best way to guard against being overcome by failure is to discipline the mind to meet failure before it arrives. This can best be accomplished by forming habits that enable one to take full possession of his mind and use it for the attainment of definite ends, on all occasions, from the smallest to the greatest daily task.

I know what your next question will be, so I will ask and answer it. You want to know how one may take full possession of his own mind. The answer to this question is the burden of this entire philosophy, as no one may take complete possession of his mind until he assimilates and puts into action all the principles of this philosophy. The starting point, as I have stated, is the adoption of a Definite Major Purpose.

The second step consists of the formation of a Master Mind alliance.

The third step consists of a form of mental discipline which we have designated as Applied Faith, the details of which we are now analyzing. Faith is the power that gives effectiveness to the other principles, and it is a state of mind that anyone can develop and use.

Before beginning the analysis of the formula through which Faith is acquired, let me remind you that there is a law known as the law of harmonious attraction, through the operation of which like attracts like. With the aid of this law the successful man either consciously or unconsciously makes his own mind success conscious by vitalizing it with a keen desire for the achievement of the object of his major purpose. It is a known fact that men of great achievement form the habit of making an obsession of their Definite Major Purpose, some well-known illustrations of which I will mention later.

HILL:

How does one go about the development of that state of mind which you mention as an obsession, Mr. Carnegie?

CARNEGIE:

It is accomplished by adopting a definite purpose or plan and backing it with a burning desire for its realization. Here the habit of repetition of thought comes into action. The habit may be developed by making the object of one's plan or purpose the dominating thought of the mind.

If the desire back of the plan or purpose is strong enough it will have the effect of calling into the mind a picture of the object of the purpose, and of dwelling upon that picture at all times when the mind is not occupied with less important subjects.

This is the way that all obsessions are developed. The more one thinks and talks of an idea or plan the nearer it comes to being an obsession. Here the Master Mind roundtable discussions become powerful factors in vitalizing one's mind with the necessary obsessional quality.

You have heard it said that a man comes, finally, to believe anything he repeats often, even though it is a falsehood. Well, this is true. The principle of repetition is the medium through which one may fan his desires into a burning flame of intensity.

Any thought that is expressed orally, and continuously repeated from day to day, through Master Mind discussions and otherwise, will be taken over by the subconscious mind eventually and carried out to its logical conclusion. All great leaders who make life pay on their own terms, through what the world commonly calls success, do so by giving orders to their own minds in the manner I have suggested. The mind can take and carry out orders, just as if it were a person, and it will act first upon one's dominating thoughts, whether or not they are given as direct orders. Thoughts of limitation and poverty will be carried out to their logical conclusion, which is poverty. The subconscious mind acts on one's thoughts without trying to modify or change their nature in the least. Moreover, it acts automatically, whether or not one is conscious of this action.

HILL:

If I understand you clearly, Mr. Carnegie, one can develop self-confidence by thinking in terms of what one desires to do and can do, and by excluding thoughts of the difficulties one may encounter carrying out one's plans. Is that correct?

CARNEGIE:

You have the idea precisely. While I was working as a laborer I heard a fellow worker say, "I hate poverty and I'll not endure it." He is still doing day labor, and lucky to have a job. You see, he fixed his mind on poverty and that is what his subconscious mind gave him.

It would have been different if he had said, "I enjoy riches and shall earn and receive them." It would have helped, too, if he had gone still one step further and described what sort of service he intended to give in return for the riches he desired.

Make no mistake about this fact—the mind brings the physical equivalent of that which it dwells upon. Brings it by the shortest, most economical and practical means available, by using every opportunity to achieve the object of one's desires.

When two or more people join the forces of their minds together and work harmoniously for the attainment of a definite purpose, they attain the object of that purpose much more quickly than they could if they worked independently.

When the leaders in a business organization begin to think, talk, and act together in a spirit of harmony they generally get that which they seek. It is true that people can talk and think themselves into anything they desire. Thoughts are things, and powerful things at that. They are more powerful when they are expressed in the words of an individual who knows exactly what he wants, and more powerful still when they are expressed in the words of a group of people who think, speak, and act together.

> *Faith develops a great leader.*
> *Fear creates a cringing follower.*

HILL:

I believe I follow your reasoning, Mr. Carnegie, and it seems sound. From what you have said I understand that when the people of a community or a nation begin to think and act together in connection with any definite objective, they soon find ways and means of attaining it. Is that your belief?

CARNEGIE:

That is not only my belief, but it is a fact. If the newspapers begin to publish stories about wars, and the people begin to think and talk of war in their daily conversations, they soon find themselves at war. People get that which their minds dwell upon, and this applies to a group or a community or a nation of people the same as to an individual.

One reason why we Americans are the richest and the freest people in the world (perhaps this is the only reason) is the fact that we think and talk and act in terms of freedom and riches. Our nation was literally born of our desire for liberty. Our history books are filled with the spirit of liberty. We have talked of liberty so much that we have it in abundance. We shall cease to have it if we stop talking and thinking about it.

If you want a fine illustration of how people get that about which they think and talk, go back to the history of this country and study the events that led up to the signing of the Declaration of Independence. Here you will discover something that most students of history overlook entirely—namely, the real source of the power that enabled George Washington's armies to win over vastly superior and better-equipped armies.

The power of which I speak is the power that began in the form of a definite purpose in the minds of a few men. It extended itself, through the Master Mind relationships of these men, until it gave this country the liberty and freedom we now enjoy. It can be traced definitely to John Hancock, Samuel Adams, and Richard Henry Lee. These three men communicated freely (mostly by correspondence), expressing their views and hopes regarding the freedom of the Colonies.

From this practice Samuel Adams conceived the idea that a mutual exchange of letters between the prominent people of the thirteen Colonies might help to bring about the coordination of effort so badly needed in connection with the solution of their problems.

Accordingly a Committee of Correspondence was organized. Observe that this move provided the way for increasing
the power of the Master Mind alliance of the three men by
adding to it men from all the Colonies. Observe, also, that these
three men did not content themselves by merely writing letters,
but they kept up the agitation by correspondence until it led, finally, to the historic meeting in Independence Hall, in Philadelphia, at which fifty-six men signed their names to the
document that was destined to give birth to a new nation, the
Declaration of Independence. They were motivated by an
active Faith.

But, before this meeting took place, Samuel Adams and John
Hancock hurriedly called a secret meeting of their close friends
for the purpose of taking appropriate steps to translate their definite purpose into terms of action. After the meeting had been
called to order, Samuel Adams locked the door, placed the key
in his pocket, and calmly told those present that it was imperative that a Congress of the Colonists be organized, and informed them that no man would be permitted to leave the
room until the decision for such a Congress had been agreed
upon. Here is more evidence of the power of active Faith.

Through the influence of Hancock and Adams the others
present were induced to agree that, through the Correspondence Committee, arrangements would be made for a meeting
of the First Continental Congress, to be held in Philadelphia on
September 5, 1774, almost two years before the actual signing
of the Declaration of Independence. Remember this date, and
remember the two determined men who brought it about, for
if there had been no decision to hold a Continental Congress
there could have been no signing of the Declaration of

Independence. Passive Faith never would have led to this daring move.

Agitation was kept up, by correspondence and by secret meetings between the members of the Master Mind alliance organized by Hancock, Adams, and Lee for almost two years, resulting at last in the famous meeting at Philadelphia in 1776. That meeting lasted for several days, during which fifty-six men (the number to which the Master Mind had, by then, grown) engaged in the most stupendous roundtable conversations known to modern civilization.

On June 7, 1776, Richard Henry Lee recognized that the time for mere conversations had come to an end and the time for action was at hand. He arose, addressed the Chair, and to the startled Assembly made this motion:

"Gentlemen, I make the motion that these United Colonies are, and of right ought to be, free and independent states, that they be absolved from all allegiance to the British Crown, and that all political connection between them and the State of Great Britain is, and ought to be, totally dissolved."

Out of that motion, based on active Faith, was born the world's greatest nation! Out of that motion was born the spirit that gave Washington's soldiers the power to win over seemingly insurmountable difficulties. Study carefully what had happened and you will see that these men devoted nearly two years of highly concentrated effort to the preparation of their minds for the performance, through active Faith, of a difficult and dangerous task.

I bring this to your attention here because it is in a similar manner that all great leaders condition their minds for unusual tasks. The spirit of self-determination did not spring into being by accident.

It was born in the minds of Samuel Adams, John Hancock, and Richard Henry Lee, and it was given life through action by the fifty-six men who signed the Declaration of Independence.

This is how men acquire self-confidence! This is an example of the method by which Faith is developed through deeds. Observe well and remember the fact that action followed the adoption of the definite purpose. Without action, plans and aims are fruitless. The three men who started America on the road to liberty and freedom made use of the selfsame principles of achievement that must be used by the successful leader in business, or in any other calling, and I think it no exaggeration to say that the spirit of self-determination which distinguishes the American people from all other people is but an extended portion of the same spirit that was born in the minds of men.

HILL:

The students of the philosophy of individual achievement may wish to know more about the application of the principles you have described. Will you, therefore, explain exactly how you applied these principles in building the great industrial empire which you have created?

CARNEGIE:

That is an excellent thought and I will act upon it by describing what happened when I converted all my holdings into the United States Steel Corporation, as that was the crowning achievement of my career.

Remember, however, that this particular transaction took place long after I had conditioned my mind on self-reliance, although the procedure followed when I decided to consolidate all my interests in the United States Steel Corporation was substantially the same as that which one less skilled than I in the application of self-reliance would have to follow to achieve success.

First: I applied the principle of Definiteness of Purpose by reaching a decision to consolidate all my steel industrial interests in one company and sell it. That decision required considerable thought, for it meant that if I sold out I would give up active work in business and thereby change my entire habits of living.

Second: Having decided to sell, I called certain members of my Master Mind group together and we spent several weeks in analysis and discussion of the values of my properties in order that I might set a fair price for my interests. We also had to work out a plan through which to find buyers for the properties, and arrange ways and means of approaching prospective buyers without placing ourselves at a great disadvantage if the buyers would know in advance that we were desirous of selling.

When finally completed, the plan represented the combined efforts of all the members of my Master Mind group who sat in on the discussions, and myself, and it was so devised that instead of our being placed in the position of offering our properties for sale we would be approached by the buyers with an offer to purchase the properties.

This we accomplished with very little maneuvering by arranging a dinner in New York City at which my chief Master Mind aide, Charlie Schwab, and a group of Wall Street bankers whom we had chosen as prospective buyers, would be guests.

It was arranged for Schwab to deliver a speech in which he painted a vivid picture of the great possibilities of such a consolidation of my steel interests into one company as we had planned. In his speech Schwab described, to the minutest detail, the operating company that was afterward formed to take over the properties, under the name of the United States Steel Corporation.

The speech had all the earmarks of being spontaneous, as Schwab made it clear that the plan he outlined could be carried out only by gaining my consent, and he gave no indication that he already had that.

The speech made such an impression that the meeting lasted into the late hours of the night, and before Schwab left, the bankers present at the meeting, including J. P. Morgan, gained from him a promise to place the proposed plan before me and do what he could to gain my consent to it. Not until long after the deal had been closed and I had been paid off did the bankers learn that the speech was carefully planned months in advance; then they turned the tables and the joke was on me when they told me that if I had asked an additional hundred million dollars for my properties they would have paid it.

HILL:

From your story I gather the fact that your confidence in your ability to sell your properties was so great that you planned every move well in advance of your knowledge as to who the actual buyers would be. Is that correct?

CARNEGIE:

Yes, every move was planned in advance, but we had a pretty good idea who our buyers would be. However, we planned this particular transaction no more carefully than we planned every business move we made in the operation of our steel industry.

Faith has sounder legs to stand upon when it is backed by definite plans.

Emphasize this point in the philosophy of individual achievement. Applied Faith is never based on blind moves. Blind Faith is something of which I know nothing. The only sort of Faith I know anything about is that which is supported by some combination of facts or reasonable assumption of facts. One of the major purposes of a Master Mind alliance is that of providing one with reliable knowledge upon which to build plans. With such knowledge in hand you can readily see how easy it is to develop that state of mind known as Faith.

HILL:

The statement that you have just made appears not to harmonize with your earlier statement that "supreme self-confidence is based on belief in Infinite Intelligence." If you do not recognize blind Faith, and have Faith only in provable facts or knowledge, how do you justify your Faith in Infinite Intelligence, since definite knowledge on this subject is difficult?

CARNEGIE:

You have made the mistake of assuming that there is no source of definite knowledge about Infinite Intelligence. As a matter of fact, the existence and the working principles of Infinite Intelligence are more easily proved than any other fact, although I am going to offer only a few reasons why I believe this to be so.

In the first place, the orderliness of all natural law and all that we know of the universe is indisputable evidence that there is back of all this a divine, universal plan, a form of intelligence far superior to that which we human beings understand.

I can see this greater intelligence working in every living thing, from the smallest blade of grass to man himself.

I can see it in the predictable movements and positions of the stars and planets, the exact positions of which can be calculated and foretold hundreds of years in advance.

I can see it in the phenomenon which brings together two small cells, each no longer than the fine point of a pin, and converts them into the marvelous machine we call man, carrying in those two small particles of energy, matter, and intelligence a portion of the ancestral qualities of man for numberless generations backward.

I can see it in the mystery that converts an acorn and a handful of soil into an oak tree, and I can see it in the matchless engineering with which the tree is so attached to the ground that it successfully defies the storms and gains its sustenance without moving from its original position on the earth.

I can see it in the symmetrical patterns and the ingenious breathing system in the leaves of the oak through which it takes from the air a portion of the food it needs for its sustenance.

I can see it in the law of physics, and in chemistry, through which may be found much evidence that matter can be neither created nor destroyed, although it can be transformed from one quality to another.

I can see it in the atoms in the steel I manufacture, and in the process through which metals are combined into what is known as steel.

There are many theories which are not provable, but Infinite Intelligence is not one of them, and I may as well here tell you that I believe the power with which we think and reason is nothing other than a minute portion of Infinite Intelligence functioning through man's brain.

It is not difficult to have Faith in Infinite Intelligence because we are literally surrounded with an inescapable mass of evidence of the existence of this intelligence. Why, every morsel of food we eat and everything we wear is produced from the soil of the earth and placed within easy grasp of every human being, through methods which no mere man can duplicate. Moreover, the intelligence through which this service to mankind is rendered is so bountiful that it provides alike for man and the animals and living creatures with lesser capacities to appropriate and use, thereby proving that Infinite Intelligence is also possessed of Infinite Wisdom.

And while we are on this subject of Infinite Intelligence may I not call your attention to the possibility, nay, the probability, that it was the wisdom of Infinite Intelligence which placed me in position to make a fortune and brought you and me together as a practical means of giving the world a workable philosophy through which men may better understand and appropriate to their own use the great bounties of every needed thing with which they have been surrounded? I wish you would give this idea some serious thought, for it is obvious that Infinite Intelligence works through the minds of men and uses the most practical natural media available for carrying out the plans of the Creator. Once you acquire this viewpoint you will be better prepared to depend upon Faith in carrying out the task I have assigned to you. Without such Faith your task will be difficult if not impossible of completion. With it you will meet no resistance you cannot overcome.

You mentioned the fact that the task I have given you calls for more self-confidence than you possess. Here, then, I am offering you a viewpoint which, if you accept it and act upon it, will provide you with a form of inspiration vastly greater than self-confidence. It will give you access to an abundance of Faith with which your success is assured even before you begin your task.

I sincerely hope that you will open your mind to the guidance of this Faith, for the job I have asked you to undertake is one which calls for no less than twenty years of research, during which you will receive little if any direct compensation for your labor.

Now, this calls for Faith, but it also serves as a dependable test of my judgment in selecting you for the task. If I have not chosen unwisely, you will perform the task I have set for you and the world will be richer because of your efforts, and you will ultimately be richer than you need to be for having rendered the service.

HILL:

Perhaps I deserve the polite reprimand you have given me, Mr. Carnegie, but allow me to explain that my enquiring into your belief on the subject of Infinite Intelligence in no way indicated my lack of such belief. I merely wanted your viewpoint on the subject, in order that I may pass it on to the students of the philosophy of individual achievement. I am glad I asked the question, for I now know the source to which I shall have to turn for self-reliance, and I agree with you that it is a dependable source.

I am only a young man, with limited experience in the ways of life, but I have lived long enough to recognize the vast evidence of Infinite Intelligence which you mention. While you were speaking, the thought was running through my mind that the human brain, with its intricate system for receiving and sending thoughts, is the greatest of all evidences of your theory that Infinite Intelligence is the real source of the power of thought. If this theory is correct, as I believe it to be, it is equally true that the greatest of all sources for the solution of our problems of life is that which is available through our own minds. Have I caught your viewpoint on this subject?

CARNEGIE:

Yes, you have; and you have done so with remarkable rapidity! Now that you have caught up with me I want to take you for a little trip into the inner workshop of my own mind, where you will be permitted to take inventory of the vast resources of the mind as I see them.

Once you have a complete perspective of the actual service the mind performs I believe you will never again lack the self-reliance to draw upon the forces available to you through your mind, for every need of life; and I believe, too, that you will have no difficulty in opening your mind, at will, for the guidance of Infinite Intelligence when you are faced by problems you cannot solve through reliance on your own reason.

These are some of the mind's vast store of riches, as I view them:

First, and I believe this peculiarity of the mind to be most significant, it is a known fact that the mind is the only thing over which an individual has complete control. Surely the Creator did not provide man with this astounding prerogative without thereby conveying the definite idea that it is man's greatest asset. It likewise involves a responsibility to use and develop this asset.

Second only to this right to control the mind is the important and equally significant fact that the mind has been wisely provided with a conscience to guide it in the use of the vast power it carries.

It is also highly significant that the mind has been carefully screened against all outside intruders, through a system that makes possible the opening and the closing of the mind at will.

It has been cleverly provided with a gateway of approach to Infinite Intelligence, through what is known as the subconscious mind; and this gateway has been so arranged that it cannot be opened for voluntary use except by the mind that has been first prepared by Faith. However, it can be opened voluntarily by Infinite Intelligence, when communication with man is necessary, and without his consent. Man's control over his own mind relates only to his conscious mind.

The mind has been provided with a faculty of imagination, wherein may be fashioned ways and means of translating hope and purpose into physical reality. Someone has said that the imagination is the workshop of the soul. Of that I am not sure, but there is evidence that it is the workshop of the conscious mind.

The mind has been provided with the stimulative capacity of desire and enthusiasm, with which man's plans and purposes may be given action through the imagination.

It has been provided with the power of will, through which both plan and purpose may be sustained indefinitely, thereby giving man adequate power to master fear and discouragement and opposition.

It has been given the capacity for Faith, through which the will and the reasoning faculty can be subdued while the entire machinery of the brain is turned over to the guiding force of Infinite Intelligence. Get the full significance of this fact and you will be near to the method by which one may develop Faith.

The mind has been cleverly prepared, through a sixth sense, for direct connection with other minds (under the Master Mind principle), from which it may add to its own power the stimulative forces of other minds that serve so effectively, at times, to stimulate the imagination.

It has been given the capacity to reason, through which facts and theories may be combined into hypotheses, ideas, and plans.

It has been given the power of deduction, by which it may foretell the future by analysis of the past. This characteristic explains why the philosopher looks backward in order to see the future.

It has been given the power to select, modify, and control the nature of its thoughts, thereby giving man the privilege of building his own character to order, and of determining what sort of thoughts shall dominate his mind.

It has been provided with a marvelous filing system for receiving, recording, and recalling every thought it has expressed, through what is called a memory. Moreover, this astonishing system automatically classifies and files related thoughts in such a manner that the recall of one particular thought leads to the recall (or memory) of its associated thoughts.

It has been given the power of emotion, of feeling, through which it can stimulate the body for any desired action, at will.

It has been given the power to function secretly, and in absolute silence, thereby insuring privacy under all circumstances. What a power!

It has an unlimited capacity to receive, organize, and store knowledge.

It has the power to aid in the maintenance of the health of the physical body, and apparently it is the main source of cure of physical ills, all other sources being merely contributory. It also keeps the physical body in repair.

It controls and directs, automatically, a marvelous system of chemistry through which it converts all food taken into the body into suitable combinations for the maintenance of the body.

It automatically operates the heart, with which the blood-stream is used to distribute food to the places where it is needed and to carry off the waste materials and the worn cells of the body.

It has the power of self-discipline, through which it can form any desired habit, or modify and change any habit, at will.

It is the common meeting ground wherein man may commune with the Creator, through prayer, by the simple process of setting aside the power of will and opening the gateway of the subconscious mind, through Faith.

It is the sole producer of every idea and every tool and every machine and every invention created by man for his convenience in the business of living in a material world.

It is the sole source of all happiness and all misery, of both poverty and riches of every nature whatsoever, and it devotes its energies to whichever of these is dominated by the power of thought.

It is the source of all human relationships, the builder of friendships, the creator of enemies, according to the manner in which it is used.

It has the power to resist and defend itself against all external conditions and circumstances, although it cannot always control these.

It has no limitations, within reason, save only those which the individual accepts through his lack of Faith! Truly, "Whatever the mind can believe, the mind can achieve."

It has the power to change from one mood to another at will; therefore it need never be damaged beyond repair.

It can relax into temporary oblivion, through sleep, and prepare itself for a fresh start, within a few hours.

It grows stronger and more dependable the more it is used.

It can convert sound into music that rests and soothes body and soul.

It can send the sound of the human voice around the earth in a fraction of a second.

It can make two blades of grass grow where only one grew before.

It can build a printing press that receives a roll of paper at one end and turns out a completely printed and bound book at the other end, in a few seconds.

It can build a skyscraper that reaches hundreds of feet into the air, and it can span the widest river with a bridge hung from small wires woven into ropes.

It can order sunlight at will, whenever desired, by merely pushing a button.

It can convert water into steam and steam into electricity.

It can control the temperature of heat at will.

It can create fire by rubbing two pieces of wood together.

It can produce music by drawing the hair from the tail of a horse across strings made from the gut of an animal.

It can accurately locate any position on the earth by the position of the stars.

It can harness the law of gravitation and make it do the work of man in a thousand different ways.

It can build a machine that will generate electricity from the air.

It can build an airplane that will safely transport human beings through the air.

It can build a machine that will penetrate the human body with light and photograph the bones without injury.

It can clear the jungle and convert the desert into a garden spot of productivity.

It can harness the waves of the ocean and convert them into power for the operation of machinery.

It can produce glass that will not break and convert wood pulp into clothing for the adornment of the body.

It can transform the stumbling blocks of failure into stepping-stones to achievement.

It can create a machine that can detect falsehoods.

It can accurately measure any circle by the smallest fragment of its arc.

It can seal hermetically any sort of food and preserve it indefinitely.

It can record and reproduce any sound, including the human voice, with the aid of a machine and a piece of wax.

It can record and reproduce any sort of color or movement of any physical body with the aid of a piece of glass and a strip of celluloid.

It can build a machine that will travel in the air, on or under the water, or on the ground.

It can build a machine that will plow its way through the thickest forest, smashing trees as though they were cornstalks.

It can build a shovel that will lift as many tons of dirt in a minute as ten men could move in a day.

It can harness the magnetic poles of the northern and the southern portions of the earth, with the aid of a compass, and determine direction accurately.

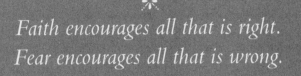

Faith encourages all that is right.
Fear encourages all that is wrong.

And yet, with all this miraculous power the majority of the people of the world permit themselves to be cowered by fears of difficulties which do not exist save in their own imaginations. The archenemy of mankind is fear!

We fear poverty in the midst of an overabundance of riches.

We fear ill health despite the ingenious system nature has provided us with which the physical body is automatically maintained in working order.

We fear criticism when there are no critics save that which we set up through our own imaginations.

We fear the loss of love of friends and relatives although we know well enough that our own conduct is sufficient to maintain love through all ordinary circumstances of human relationships.

We fear old age, whereas we should accept it as a medium of greater wisdom and understanding.

We fear the loss of liberty although we know that liberty is a matter of harmonious relationship with others.

We fear death when we know it is inevitable, therefore beyond our control.

We fear failure, not recognizing that every failure carries with it the seed of an equivalent benefit.

And we feared the lightning until Franklin and Edison and a few other rare individuals who dared to take possession of their own minds proved that it is nothing but a form of energy which can be harnessed and used for the benefit of mankind.

Instead of opening our minds for the guidance of Infinite Intelligence, through Faith, we close our minds tightly with every conceivable shade and degree of limitation, based upon our unnecessary fears.

We know that man is the master of every other living thing on earth, yet we fail to look about us and learn from the birds of the air and the beasts of the jungle that even the dumb animals have been wisely provided with food and the necessities of their existence, through the divine plan which makes all fear unnecessary.

We complain of lack of opportunity and cry out against those who dare to take possession of their own minds, not recognizing that every man who has a sound mind has the right and the power to provide himself with every material thing he needs or can use.

We fear the discomfort of pain, not recognizing that pain is a universal language through which man is warned of evils that need correction.

Because of our fears we go to the Creator with prayers over petty details we could and should settle for ourselves, then give up and lose Faith when we do not get the results we ask for, not recognizing our duty to offer prayers of thanks for the blessings we already possess.

We talk and preach sermons about sin, failing to recognize that the greatest of all sins is that of loss of Faith in an all-wise Creator who has provided His children with more blessings than any earthly parent ever thinks of providing for his own children.

We convert the revelations of invention into tools of destruction through what we politely call "war." Then we cry out in protest when the law of Compensation properly punishes us with a depression.

We speak of the animals of the jungle as "dumb beasts," failing to recognize that despite their "dumbness" they do not engage in wars and have no depressions.

We profane our minds with envy, greed, avarice, jealousy, lust, and fear, then wonder why Faith does not bestow its beneficence upon us, not recognizing that Faith will no more fraternize with these states of mind than will oil and water mix.

You ask me, "How may one develop Faith?" I'll tell you how. Faith may be developed by clearing the mind of its enemies. Clear the mind of negative thoughts and fears and self-imposed limitations and lo! Faith has filled the place without effort. If you cannot take my word for this, try it for yourself and be forever convinced.

I repeat, there is no great mystery about the state of mind known as Faith. Give it a place to dwell and it will move in without ceremony or invitation. Stop talking about Faith and start practicing it. What could be more simple? Who is so short-sighted as not to recognize the simplicity and the soundness of the approach to Faith I have described?

We preach sermons and offer up prayers in the name of God, yet we rarely make more than a gesture at following His admonition for us to liquidate our problems through the simple state of mind known as Faith.

We build great edifices of worship in the name of God, yet we profane them with minds that are steeped in fear and self-imposed limitations which He clearly promised us we need not endure.

If I seem to speak plainly, be assured it is because I feel that mankind needs the quickening influence of plain speech to shock people into recognizing that everything they need or want is already within their grasp. All they need to do is to take possession of their own minds and use them! To do this man has no one to consult except himself. The approach to liberty, freedom, and abundance of the material necessities and luxuries of life is through the individual's mind. This mind is the only thing over which he has complete control, yet it is the one thing he so seldom uses intelligently.

Take my message to the students of the philosophy of achievement. Translate it for them in the same burning words in which I have delivered it to you. Never mind about those who will not agree with me, but deliver the message unabridged, for the benefit of those who are ready to hear the truth and are willing to appropriate and use it!

Once in a great while the world is blessed by the presence of one who takes control of his mind and uses it for the good of mankind. Then it has found a genius; an Edison, an Aristotle, a Plato, or a great leader in thought and in action in some field of useful endeavor.

Marconi took possession of his own mind and used it to reveal the principle of wireless communication.

Edison's mind gave the world the incandescent electric lamp and a hundred other useful devices for the benefit of mankind.

Copernicus and Bruno took possession of their minds and gave the world the telescope, and a look into the starry heaven, millions of miles beyond the range of the unaided human eye.

Columbus took possession of his mind and gave us a new world which now serves as the last frontier of human liberty and freedom.

Orville and Wilbur Wright took possession of their minds and gave man wings and mastery of the air.

Johann Gutenberg took possession of his mind and gave us movable type, and thereby made possible every book we possess, and gave us the means of preserving the accumulated experience of mankind for the benefit of the yet unborn generations.

Robert Fulton took possession of his mind and gave us mastery of the seas, through the steamboat.

Henry Ford took possession of his own mind and gave us a dependable vehicle of rapid transportation, at a price within reach of the humblest person.

Theodore Roosevelt took possession of his mind and gave us the Panama Canal, providing a valuable measure of protection for our shores against attack by enemies from other countries.

Eli Whitney took possession of his mind and gave a measure of economic security to the people of the Southern states, through the perfection of the modern cotton gin.

Stephen Foster took possession of his mind, temporarily, and gave us songs that enrich our souls.

Emerson took possession of his mind and enriched the world with his essays on compensation, self-reliance, and other subjects.

Newton took possession of his mind and revealed the law of gravitation that keeps the stars and planets properly related and confined to their accustomed places in the universe.

Samuel Adams, John Hancock, and Richard Henry Lee took possession of their minds and inspired the movement which gave America its boasted liberty of thought and freedom of action.

Omar Khayyam took possession of his mind and gave the world, through the Rubaiyat, great poetic thought.

Samuel Morse took possession of his mind and gave the world the modern system of telegraphy, and Alexander Graham Bell took possession of his mind and gave us the modern telephone.

Cyrus McCormick took possession of his mind and gave us the reaper, with its manifold benefits to agriculture.

James J. Hill took possession of his mind and brought the East and West into easy accessibility to one another, through a great railway system.

And, if I may be pardoned for personal references to my own work, I had to take possession of my own mind to give America the United States Steel Corporation.

These are well-known examples of self-reliance based on Faith!

Let us learn from these outstanding examples of achievement one great lesson we all need to know, and that is the obvious fact that self-reliance and Faith are based on Definiteness of Purpose, backed by definite plans of action!

The best way to start developing Faith is by choosing an objective and beginning at once to attain it, through whatever media available. Procrastination and Faith have nothing in common.

Our greatest weakness is our failure to take possession of our minds and use them.

Let us hope that someday, and soon, some person, perhaps some unknown person, will come up from obscurity, will arise, take possession of his own mind, and inspire the American people to make a fuller and better use of the great American privilege of liberty and freedom that we possess.

Somewhere in the United States that person may now be preparing himself for this very job. Perhaps he is being tested through hardship, disappointment, and discouragement, as practically all other great leaders of thought have been conditioned for their work.

And still other unknowns may yet come forth from the great American melting pot and inspire the people to make better use of the abundance of opportunities with which they have been blessed.

Through the leadership of these as yet unknown men we will be given:

A more practical system of education.

A more practical application of religion.

Common decency in the field of politics.

Greater safety in automobile and airplane traffic.

Better working relationships between employers and employees.

Improved methods of farming and marketing farm products.

An effective antidote against the growing evil of alcoholic drink.

Better public health facilities for all our people.

A cure for the common cold.

A cure for cancer.

A workable plan for settling international disputes without resort to war.

A more effective control of crime, and a workable plan for eliminating many of our present criminal factors through preventative measures.

A more equitable distribution of the tax burden.

More effective means of collecting taxes economically.

Ways and means of eliminating waste in governmental management.

Schools of diplomacy and statesmanship in which men who seek public office will be prepared for their duties.

Cheaper and better homes and adequate housing for every citizen.

New and cheaper fuel for automobiles.

An advertising department for every state, to publicize its assets.

Some appropriate reward for the leaders of industry, to take the place of the brickbats and epithets with which they are greeted all too often.

These are but a few morsels of food for the imagination of men and women who wish to develop self-reliance through useful effort. Those who avail themselves of these and other opportunities for self-development in America must take possession of their own minds and rely upon themselves. They must accept the fact that the mind has the power to convert failures into success. That it is the master of imagination, vision, enthusiasm, initiative, and all forms of human endeavor.

And they must recognize the fact that the mind can travel from one part of the universe to another at will; it grows stronger and more dependable with use; it can read Nature's Bible as it has been written in the geological surfaces of the earth and thereby accurately measure millions of years of the earth's history; it is free to all who use it; it clothes itself in the physical equivalent of its dominating thoughts; it is the unchallenged master of every living creature below the intelligence of man; it can harness and use the laws of nature in a thousand useful ways; it can analyze and interpret the contents and mass of the sun, ninety-three million miles away, through mathematical calculation and analysis of the sun's rays.

In brief, the development of Faith is largely a matter of understanding the astounding power of the mind as the source of that power that has been revealed through these and other unquestionable sources of evidence.

One of man's difficulties in connection with the under-standing of Faith has been the fallacy of clothing it in mystery, whereas the only real mystery about it is man's failure to make use of it!

We have done too much preaching and too little practicing of Faith. I speak from personal experience when I say that Faith is a state of mind which can be acquired and used effectively and as easily as any other state of mind. It is all a matter of under-standing and application. Truly, "Faith without works is dead." It is also impossible, for how can one express Faith except by action?

My early days of youth were cursed by poverty and limi-tation of opportunity, a fact with which all who know me are acquainted. I am no longer cursed by poverty because I took possession of my mind, and that mind has yielded to me every material thing I want, and much more than I need. Faith is no patented right of mine! It is a universal power as available to the humblest person as it is to the greatest.

HILL:

Your description of the possibilities of the human mind is both interesting and revealing, Mr. Carnegie. In all the reading I have done in connection with the subject of psychology and the working principles of the mind I found nothing that ap-proaches, even approximately, your description of the powers of the mind. Where did you acquire all this knowledge?

CARNEGIE:

What knowledge I have of the powers of the mind I acquired from the greatest of all schools, the University of Life! It has been a habit of mine, extending backward over many years, to devote a certain amount of time daily to silent meditation and thought in connection with the plan and purpose and working principles of the mind.

Some might call this habit "getting in tune with the Infinite." At any rate it is a habit I shall continue as long as I live, and I heartily recommend it to all who wish to become better acquainted with the powers of their own minds.

We have, in America, the finest system of public schools to be found anywhere. We have the finest buildings and the best of equipment. We have learned men and women teachers. We teach everything imaginable except the practical art of making a living through the application of the knowledge gained in school. It is my hope that the Philosophy of American Achievement will find its way into the public schools and become a helpful factor in eliminating this objectionable deficiency in the public school system, by offering the secret of mental discipline.

HILL:

Through your analysis of the powers of the mind I have observed that you emphasized the importance of action as a means of developing self-reliance. Have you anything to add to that which you have already said on this subject, Mr. Carnegie?

CARNEGIE:

Just this: There can be no perfect example of self-reliance that is not expressed in terms of action. It is true that the mind influences one's deeds; but the principle is reciprocal, for one's deeds influence one's mind. Evidence of this fact may be found in the experience of a child that is learning to walk. At first the mind guides the steps through many wobbles and tumbles, but after a while coordination between the mind and the movement of the legs takes place, and walking becomes almost an automatic procedure. So it is with the relationships between the mind and physical action. The mind influences action and action influences the mind. Perfection is reached when the two become balanced in a state of complete coordination.

Another example of the same principle is the musician learning to play an instrument. Perfection is attained only after physical practice establishes coordination between the mind and the movement of the fingers. In no other way can one become proficient in music.

I heard an accomplished pianist say that the keyboard of the piano has been so perfectly painted in her mind that she could play as well in the dark as when she looked at the keyboard. She attained self-reliance in connection with her music in precisely the same way that one must attain self-reliance in connection with anything else, by coordination of effort between the mind and the physical body. One has no difficulty in developing Faith in connection with that which one does through well-established habit, because habit is nothing more nor less than coordination between the faculties of the mind and the physical body.

HILL:

Summing up the subject of Faith in one sentence, then, would you say: "It is the art of believing by doing?"

CARNEGIE:

That would be a very accurate way of stating the matter. But you should emphasize the fact that the "doing" must become a fixed habit, as Faith is a state of mind which remains only as long as it is exercised through use. You can develop a strong arm by giving it unusual, regular exercise. But it will assume its regular size if the exercise is discontinued. It is the same with the mental attitude known as Faith.

Two words are inseparably associated with the development of Faith. They are "persistence" and "action." To these two might be added a third, "repetition." Perfection in the exercise of Faith is only a matter of placing persistence and action behind Definiteness of Purpose, with strong emphasis on the action. Here you have as simple a definition of the method of developing Faith as I could offer. Examination of the definition will show that Faith is within easy reach of all who will appropriate it.

HILL:

Mr. Carnegie, may I assume, from all you have said on the subject of Faith, that it is a state of mind which can best be attained by some form of individual action that is related to known facts or recognized realities?

From your analysis of the subject of Faith, and your emphasis on the importance of moving with Definiteness of Purpose in order to achieve a desired objective, I have reached the conclusion that you believe Faith can best be attained where one is inspired to action by a definite motive, based on tangible evidence of facts or a reasonable hypothesis assuming the existence of facts.

Nowhere in your analysis have you indicated your belief that one can have or that one should have Faith in anything one cannot comprehend through the ordinary faculties of understanding. I may have misunderstood you. Will you, therefore, state specifically whether or not it is your belief that anyone can have Faith in something with which he is not familiar, and concerning the existence of which he is not certain?

CARNEGIE:

You wish to know whether or not one may have Faith in anything concerning the existence of which one does not have proof, or a reasonable hypothesis of proof. The answer to this is unavoidably and definitely "No!" To ask one to believe in or have Faith in anything one cannot comprehend, through the faculty of reason, would be as unreasonable as to ask a blind man, who had never seen any colors, to describe the colors of the rainbow! He simply could not do it. There would be no place where he could begin; no method by which he could offer a description by comparison.

Faith is a state of mind which can be attained only by definite action in connection with a definite motive. Desire and motive clear the mind of many negatives which must be removed before Faith can be developed. If a man desires anything to be true, and persists in his desire through action, he soon finds his mind opening automatically for guidance through Faith, provided always that he believes he can get the object of his desire.

Christians have a definite approach to an understanding of how the principle of Faith works by studying the words and deeds of Christ. He did not recommend a passive attitude toward Faith, but He did demonstrate its power through works, the results of which were so astounding they could be explained only through Faith.

Christ demonstrated the power of Faith by raising the dead, walking on water, feeding the multitudes on five fishes, curing the sick, and healing the blind. He asked no one to believe these things were possible through passive Faith; but He made definite demonstrations through which He proved the power of an active Faith backed by deeds. Here, then, is the answer to your question as how one may develop Faith.

First, adopt a definite purpose and create a plan for its attainment. The presence of a plan connotes action.

Second, form an alliance with other people, under the Master Mind principle, and begin at once to carry out the plan. In this stage of the procedure the action becomes greatly intensified, through the multiplicity of minds engaged in it. This is precisely the procedure followed by Christ.

Third, master and apply the principle of Applied Faith (still more action), this being a prescribed rule of conduct that can be easily complied with if one has prepared the way adequately, through the preceding steps.

By the time the third step has been taken, the individual will not need further instructions on how to develop Faith, for he will already possess it.

I have never known of Faith bringing practical results through any method other than that which I have here explained. Faith has worked in my behalf many times, but always I have done my part, through some plan or some form of action on my part.

I had such Faith in the consummation of the organization of the United States Steel Corporation, and in the object of that organization, that I saw the transaction a completed reality before I made my plans known to the men who supplied the money for that corporation. But my Faith was the result of weeks of careful planning and coaching of members of my Master Mind group in the part each was to play in the transaction, all of which called for the most intense action of my business career.

In Hebrews, chapter 11, first verse, we find this statement:

"Faith is the substance of things hoped for, the evidence of things not seen."

Here we find supporting evidence of the statement that strong motive or desire may lead to the state of mind known as Faith. Following this quotation from the Bible is a series of illustrations of the power of Faith through deeds, thus clearly showing that the reference to Faith connotes an active Faith.

Study the lives of all great leaders—those who are known to have been inspired by enduring Faith in the attainment of their desires—and you will discover that they were men of action. I know nothing of any sort of Faith that will produce desirable results without action.

> *Anything that causes one to be afraid should have close examination.*

HILL:

Now, Mr. Carnegie, I am going to ask another very definite question, and in doing so I want you to know, before you answer, that I am moved to ask this question only by the most profound desire for dependable knowledge, something on which I can lean with reasonable assurance of its soundness and its practicability.

My question is this: How is one to have Faith in Infinite Intelligence unless one can find reasonable proof of the existence of such a power? If there is such a power, what is its source?

Where does it exist? How may one avail one's self of this power if it exists?

CARNEGIE:

Evidence of the existence of Infinite Intelligence is so abundant that its existence is the easiest thing in the world to prove.

I hold here in my hand an ordinary watch which measures time accurately. I know who made the watch. I understand the principle of its operation. I know something of the metal of which it is made, even down to the molecules of that metal.

I also know that if I take the parts of this watch, disassociate them from their organized relationship to each other, put them in my hat, and shake them, they would not and could not reassemble themselves into the working machine we know as a watch—not even if they were shaken aimlessly for millions of years.

The watch operates accurately only because there is organized intelligence and a definite plan for its operation back of it.

I know, with equal Faith, that there is an organized Master Intelligence back of the marvelous plan of operation of the universe.

I sincerely trust this answers your questions satisfactorily. The only additional suggestion I can offer which may be of help to you and the students of the philosophy of individual achievement is this: Faith in Infinite Intelligence is something every man must acquire for himself, and the only practical method of doing so is that which I have described, by close examination of the perceivable evidences of its existence, as they are available through the known facts and realities of that portion of the world about us with which we are familiar, and by meditation, analysis, and thought.

I would stress the importance of silent meditation. Through this form of thought one quickens the subconscious mind and makes it more active in serving as a connecting link between the conscious mind of man and Infinite Intelligence. In this statement may be found the clue by which many people may discover how to take possession of their own minds.

In the hurry and rush of this materialistic age most people are apt to neglect the all-important habit of communing with themselves, through silence!

Every person should have a definite period of not less than one hour out of every twenty-four, during which he confines his mind to introspective analysis of himself and his relationship to the world in which he lives. This form of meditation will yield stupendous dividends of knowledge, and it will lead to an easy acceptance of the reality of the fact that every mind is but a tiny reflection of Infinite Intelligence.

Here I must leave the subject of Infinite Intelligence with you and the students of this philosophy. I have given you all the information on the subject that I possess. From this point you and all others who acquire a workable understanding of Faith must accept the responsibility strictly on your own. Whatever additional information you wish, you must seek within your own minds, through meditation and thought!

ANALYSIS OF CHAPTER ONE

By Napoleon Hill

From Mr. Carnegie's analysis of the subject of Faith it becomes obvious that the state of mind known as Faith is something that can be attained only by a proper conditioning of the mind, by clearing it of all negative thoughts. On this point he is very definite!

After the mind has been cleared of negative thoughts, there are three simple steps one must take in creating the state of mind known as Faith, viz.:

1. Form a definite desire based upon an appropriate motive for its attainment.
2. Create a definite plan for the attainment of the desire.
3. Begin action in carrying out the plan, subordinating all other endeavors to its successful attainment.

These steps, persistently pursued, will take one as far as one can go alone. From there on, the subconscious mind must be relied upon to take over one's plans and carry them out to their logical conclusion or one must substitute entirely new plans for the attainment of one's objective.

When I speak of "conditioning" one's mind for the successful development of Faith, I have reference to the complete elimination of all fear, doubt, and indecision. The conditioning process begins always with Definiteness of Purpose based on a burning desire for its achievement.

Faith is a state of mind wherein one temporarily sets aside his own reason and willpower, and opens his mind completely for the guidance of Infinite Intelligence, for the attainment of some definite desire. The guidance takes place in the form of an idea or a plan that is presented to the conscious mind through the faculty of imagination.

Action is an essential of Faith. Words without deeds will be fruitless. Hence desire should be accompanied by a definite plan for the attainment of its objective. If the first plan adopted proves to be unsound, supplant it with another, and continue doing this until the right plan is found. Persistence must accompany action.

The object of one's desire must, to induce the state of mind known as Faith, be so definite that one can see it as an already attained reality. Instead of praying for the object of the desire, reverse this rule and give thanks for having already received it. Repeat this procedure daily.

Never mind what your reason tells you of the impracticability of this procedure. Remember, you have temporarily overridden your faculty of reason, in order to give Infinite Intelligence an opportunity to guide you. Unless you can carry out this instruction willingly, you have not subordinated your reason to the higher power of Infinite Intelligence. Remember this! And be guided accordingly.

"Faith," said a great philosopher, "is the courage of the mind which plunges ahead and is confident of finding truth. This Faith is not the enemy of reason, but rather its torch; it is the Faith of Christopher

Columbus and Galileo, demanding proof and counterproof—*provando e riprovando*—the only faith possible at the present time."

This procedure places one's religious strength squarely back of one's desires and thereby hands the problem over to the Creator! When the solution of the problem comes, as come it will if one relies entirely upon Faith for guidance, it will come in the form of an idea or plan that will be presented to the conscious mind.

The soundness of the plan, and the authenticity of its source, will be manifested by the intensity of enthusiasm that accompanies it. When the plan comes, act on it at once.

Repetition of thought in connection with the object of one's desires is the secret of success. The subconscious mind comes, finally, to accept and act upon any idea submitted to it repeatedly, in the form of a definite desire. Never mind how this is done. Do your part by following these instructions with the same simplicity of Faith with which a child follows the direction of its parents and you will not be disappointed.

It is not your responsibility nor anyone's to demand of Infinite Intelligence an explanation as to how it works or why. Your responsibility ends with the faithful carrying-out of these instructions.

This suggested procedure has nothing whatsoever to do with any dogma or creed. It does not interfere in the slightest with any religion, although it has much in common with all religions founded on the power of Faith.

If your plans do not mature when you expect them to, repeat the procedure here recommended until they do yield results. If you have Faith, you cannot fail—provided, of course, your objective is right and sound. To doubt this is the equivalent of doubting the power of the Creator. The working principle of Faith is as definite and as precise as the power that holds the stars and planets suspended in space. It cannot fail if you open your mind completely for its guidance.

To carry out these instructions you need no permission. The only help you need is that which you may receive from your own conscience. Make sure, however, that your conscience serves as your guide and not as your conspirator.

In carrying out these instructions, be willing to do your part. Decide what you want, create a plan for attaining it, then move at once to put the plan into operation. If you receive a "hunch" to change or modify your plan, act on it. Remember that Infinite Intelligence may have better plans than any you can create. Give it the benefit of the doubt. If it presents to your mind a better plan than the one you have adopted, you will recognize the superior plan by the impulse of enthusiasm which will accompany it.

Do not expect Infinite Intelligence to bring you the physical equivalent of that which you desire. Be satisfied with a plan with which you can acquire the object of your desires through the recognized rules of human relationship. Do not look for miracles. Infinite Intelligence works through natural laws, using the most available means for carrying out your desires.

Do not expect something for nothing. Be willing to give an equivalent value for all that you desire, and include in your plans a definite provision for doing so. Do not desire something to which you are not rightfully entitled. Infinite Intelligence frowns on the cutting of corners and sharp practices. Anything you acquire by such practices will be of no enduring value to you.

Examine your motives and desires carefully, to make sure they contemplate no injustices to others. Injustice sets up a counterforce of opposition that will be stronger than your desire. Unjust motives may appear to prevail for the moment, but eventually they can bring only disaster. Evidence of this truth may be found in the history of every person who has started out to conquer the world. Apparently the Creator has no need for world conquerors, or else someone would have succeeded.

Place yourself on the side of right at the beginning, by planning to give an equivalent value for everything you expect to receive. If you neglect to observe this instruction, do not blame your failure on the lack of the power of Faith. Blame it on your own lack of understanding Faith.

Faith is the strongest power known to man, but no one has known of this or any other power ever having caused any natural law to be suspended. Do not, therefore, expect Faith to give you any advantage based on injustice to others; and do not expect it to give you something for nothing, or something for less than its value. All the evidence available to man indicates definitely that such expectations are not in harmony with the Creator's will.

Be generous in giving credit to those who cooperate with you. The Creator may not demand this, but those who lend you their cooperation will appreciate it. Selfishness and greed are not related to Faith. Neither are vanity and super-selfish egotism. Humility of the heart is definitely related to Faith. To be truly great, one must first be sincerely humble.

Personal pride often is vanity or super-selfish egotism misnamed. Be careful, therefore, of all plans based on what you may believe to be personal pride, lest they contain an element of irritation that will antagonize others and attract their unfriendly opposition.

Be definite in your plans; be persistent in their pursuit; be courageous and self-reliant; but also be mindful of the rights and the feelings of others, and express this state of mind in a spirit of true humility if you expect friendly cooperation from other people.

HOW I DISCOVERED EVIDENCE OF THE POWER OF INFINITE INTELLIGENCE

> ✳
>
> *In every man there is something*
> *wherein I may learn of him,*
> *and in that I am his pupil.*
>
> —RALPH WALDO EMERSON

I invite you to share with me a stupendous fortune; a fortune which I had been accumulating over a long period of years without knowing that I possessed it.

The strangest feature of these riches which I wish to share with you is the fact that I can profit most by sharing them with others!

I began, unconsciously, to accumulate this wealth when I entered the oldest of all colleges—the *college of adversity.*

During the "business depression" I took a postgraduate course in this college. It was then that I uncovered my hidden fortune. I made the discovery one morning when notice came that my bank had closed its doors, possibly never again to be opened, for it was then that I began to take inventory of intangible and unused assets.

Come with me while I describe what the inventory disclosed.

Let us begin with the most important item on the list: *Faith!*

When I looked into my own heart I found that, despite my financial loss, I had left an abundance of Faith in Infinite Intelligence and in my fellow men. Along with this discovery came another of greater importance, the discovery that with *Faith* one can accomplish that which not all the money in the world can achieve.

When I was possessed of all the money I needed, I made the grievous error of believing money to be a permanent source of *power*. Now came the astonishing revelation that money, without *Faith*, is but so much inert matter, and of itself possessed of no power whatsoever.

Realizing, perhaps for the first time in my life, the stupendous *power* of enduring Faith, I analyzed myself very carefully to determine just how much of this form of riches I possessed.

I began by taking a walk into the woods. I wanted to get away from the crowd, away from the noise of the city, away from the disturbances of "civilization," so I could meditate and *think*.

On my journey I picked up an acorn and held it in the palm of my hand. I found it at the roots of a giant oak tree from which it had fallen. I judged the age of the tree to be so great that it must have been a fair-sized tree when George Washington was a small boy.

As I stood there looking at that great tree, and its small embryonic offspring which I held in my hand, I realized that the tree had grown from a small acorn. I realized, too, that all the men living on the earth could not together build a tree like that one. I was conscious of the fact that some form of intangible intelligence had caused the acorn, from which the tree had sprung, to germinate and grow.

I picked up a handful of black soil and covered the acorn with it. I now held in my hand the equivalent of the visible portion of the sum and substance out of which that magnificent tree had grown. I could see and feel the soil and the acorn, but I could neither see nor feel the *intelligence* which had created a great tree out of these simple substances. *But I had Faith that such intelligence existed.* Moreover, I knew it to be a form of intelligence such as no living being possessed.

At the root of the giant oak I plucked a fern. Its leaves were beautifully designed—yes, designed—and I realized as I looked at the fern that it, too, was created by the same *intelligence* which had produced the oak tree.

49

I continued my walk in the woods until I came to a running brook of clear, rippling water. By this time I was tired, so I took a seat near the brook that I might rest and listen to its rhythmic music, as it danced on its way back to the sea.

The experience brought back sweet memories of my youth, when I had played by the side of a similar brook. As I sat there listening to the music of that little stream I became conscious of an unseen being—an *intelligence* which spoke to me from within and told me the enchanting story of *water*, and this is the story:

"Water! Pure, cool water. The same water that has been rendering service ever since this planet cooled off and became the home of man, beast, and vegetation.

"Water! Ah, what a story you could tell if you spoke man's language. You have quenched the thirst of endless millions of earthly wayfarers; you have fed the flowers; you have expanded into steam and have turned the wheels of man's machinery, condensing and going back again into your original form. You have cleaned the sewers and have washed the pavements, returning to your source, there to purify yourself and start all over again.

"When you move you travel in one direction only—toward the great oceans from whence you came. You are forever going and coming, but you seem always to be happy at your labor.

"Water! Clean, pure, sparkling water! No matter how much dirty work you perform, you cleanse yourself at the end of your labors. Imperishable water. You cannot be created nor can you be destroyed. You are akin to life. Without your beneficence no form of life could exist."

I had heard a great sermon, a sermon which yielded to me the secret of the music of the running brook. I had seen and felt added evidence of that same *intelligence* which created the great oak tree from a tiny acorn.

The shadows of the trees were becoming longer; the day was coming to an end. As the sun slowly lowered itself beyond the western horizon I realized that it, too, had played a part in that marvelous sermon which I had heard.

Without the beneficent aid of the sun, there could have been no conversion of the acorn into an oak tree. Without the sun's help the sparkling water of the flowing brook would have remained eternally imprisoned in the oceans, and life on this earth could never have existed.

These thoughts gave a beautiful climax to the sermon I had heard; thoughts of the romantic affinity existing between the sun and water beside which all other forms of romance seemed incomparable.

I picked up a small white pebble which had been neatly polished by the rippling water of the brook. As I held it in my hand I received, from within, another and a still more impressive sermon. The *intelligence* which conveyed that truth to my conscious mind seemed to say:

"Behold, mortal, a miracle which you hold in your hand. I am only a tiny pebble of stone, yet I am, in reality, a small universe. I appear to be dead and motionless, but the appearance is deceiving. I am made of molecules. Inside my molecules are myriads of atoms. Inside the atoms are countless numbers of electrons which move at an inconceivable rate of speed. I am not a dead mass of stone. I am an organized group of units of ceaseless motion. I appear to be a solid, but the appearance is an illusion, for my electrons are separated from one another by a distance greater than their mass."

The thought conveyed by that climax was so illuminating, it held me spellbound, for I knew that I held in my hand an infinitesimal portion of the energy which keeps the sun and the stars and the little earth on which we live in their respective places.

Meditation revealed to me the beautiful reality that there was law and order even in the small confines of the tiny pebble I held in my hand. I realized that within the mass of that pebble the romance and reality of nature were affinitized. I realized, too, that within the small stone which I held in my hand, fact transcended fancy.

Never before had I felt so keenly the significance of the evidence of natural law and order and purpose which are wrapped up in a tiny bit of stone. Never before had I felt myself so near the source of my *Faith* in Infinite Intelligence.

It was a beautiful experience out there in the midst of Mother Nature's family of trees and running brooks, where the very calmness bade my weary soul to be quiet and to look, feel, and listen while Infinite Intelligence unfolded to me the story of its reality.

For the moment I was in another world. This was a world which knew nothing of "business depressions" and bank failures and struggle for existence and competition between men.

Never, in all my life, had I previously been so overwhelmingly conscious of the real evidence of Infinite Intelligence, nor of the causes of my *Faith* therein.

I lingered in this newly found paradise until the Evening Star began to twinkle; then reluctantly I retraced my footsteps back to the city, there to mingle once more with those who are driven by the inexorable rules of "civilization" in a mad scramble for existence.

I am now back in my study, with my books; but I am swept by a feeling of loneliness and a longing to be out there by the side of that friendly brook where, only a few hours ago, I bathed my soul in the soothing reality of Infinite Intelligence.

Yes, I know now that my *Faith* in Infinite Intelligence is real and enduring. It is not a blind faith; it is a Faith based upon close examination of the handiwork of this intelligence.

I had been looking for evidence of the source of my Faith in the wrong direction; I had been seeking it in the deeds of men. I found it in a tiny acorn and a giant oak tree—in the leaflets of a humble fern and in the soil of the earth; in the friendly sun which warms the earth and gives motion to the waters; in a tiny pebble of stone and in the Evening Star; in the silence and the calm of the great outdoors.

> *Faith constructs; fear tears down.*
> *The order never is reversed.*

I am moved to suggest that Infinite Intelligence reveals itself through silence more readily than through the boisterousness of men's struggles in their mad rush to accumulate things material.

My bank account had vanished, my bank had collapsed, but I was still richer than most millionaires because I had *Faith*, and with this I can accumulate other bank accounts and acquire whatever I may need to sustain myself in this maelstrom of activity known as "civilization."

Nay, I am richer than most millionaires because I depend upon a source of inspired power which reveals itself to me from within, while many of the wealthy men find it necessary to turn, for power and stimulation, to the stock ticker. My source of power is as free as the air I breathe. To avail myself of it at will I need only *Faith*, and this I have in abundance.

AN EXPERIENCE THAT LED TO REVELATION OF THE POWER OF FAITH

I shall now describe the most dramatic experience of my entire labor of research in the field of causes of success and failure.

This true story is intimately associated with a type of personal experience in connection with which no one would wish to exaggerate or treat lightly any of the details.

The story concerns my son Blair, the second of three sons. I have been left no choice but to relate the story, even though it is highly personal for mention.

After all, I am a student of life, and my time has been, and will continue to be, devoted to the study of the causes by which people may avoid poverty and misery.

I feel compelled to describe my experience with Blair because his entire life has, almost miraculously, provided evidence of the manner in which the law of Faith can be made to work in the practical affairs of life.

I shall have to go back to the time of Blair's birth to give an accurate picture of the beginning of this colorful life drama. As the story unfolds I want you to notice that Blair's case provides evidence of the irresistible power of Faith.

Keep this thought in mind and the story will be its own explanation of why I crossed the sacred threshold of family relationship for evidence with which to convey the nature and method of operation of one of nature's inexorable laws.

Blair came into this world without physical ears. He did not have even the outer signs of ears, and subsequent X-ray examinations by noted physicians disclosed the fact that he did not have even as much as an opening in the skull. The doctors in attendance at his birth took me aside and told me as gently as possible that the child would never hear or speak!

"He will hear," I replied, "and he will speak!"

What made me throw back at the doctors such a seemingly foolish challenge is something I will never know, but I can describe (and this description is important) how I felt when I did so. The feeling came over me, when I heard the uncompromising opinion of finality of the doctors, that nothing was impossible! For years I had been lecturing to others, telling them, without any qualifications whatever, two very definite beliefs of mine, viz.:

1. With every adversity comes the seed of an equivalent advantage. There never has been and there probably never will be an exception to this rule because it is a part of nature's own plan, as described by Emerson in his essay on compensation.

2. The only real limitation is the one we establish in our own minds, through lack of Faith. Whatever limitations the mind establishes, the mind can also eliminate.

I had been emphasizing these two statements for years, but now I was forced to meet a factual circumstance in the form of a newly born baby with an irreparable physical affliction which seemed to knock the very foundation from under both of these rules.

It was the most dramatic experience of my life. On the one hand I saw physical evidence of limitation which apparently no mind had created and no mind could eliminate. Also I saw physical evidence of a newly born baby handicapped by a form of adversity which, as far as any reasoning mind could evaluate, could never yield "the seed of an equivalent advantage."

"What advantage," some silent voice of mockery asked, "could there possibly be to a human being born with no ears and condemned, therefore, to eternal deprivation of hearing and speech?"

The answer to that challenge was not forthcoming as far as my reasoning mind was concerned, but something inside me, some other form of intelligence with a more optimistic trend and an affinity for Faith, answered the challenge in no uncertain terms. The answer assumed a form of thought which ran something like this:

"I do not know at this time what seed of advantage there is in being born without ears, but I do know there is an equivalent advantage and I shall find it."

I did not at the time of Blair's birth, nor at any time afterward, accept in my own mind the physical reality of a child condemned hopelessly to loss of hearing and speech. I moved on the theory—to me it was more than a theory—that sometime, somehow, I would find "the seed of an advantage equivalent to the handicap" brought over by the earless child, and that I would help him cause the seed to germinate and grow to some practical advantage sufficient to compensate him for his lack of ears.

As this dramatic story is unfolded you will observe, as clearly as you can see your own face in a mirror, that: (1) I established in my own mind the mental image of a condition that would give Blair the use of hearing and speech, and (2) this image was taken over by some unknown natural law and translated into a physical reality.

The evidence is indisputable, and fortunately it is of such a nature that no one is under the necessity of accepting my statements as the only means of verifying the facts concerning the case. No fewer than fifty other people, consisting of doctors who examined Blair from time to time, teachers who gave him instruction in school, and other close associates and relatives, are as familiar as I with all but one important feature of the case. I am the only person who created a mental impulse of thought, at the time of Blair's birth, which reflected a correction of his deficiency, and I am the only person who nursed that thought continuously through Faith, until it found a way to manifest itself in physical form. You will have to accept my word for this part of the story. Everything else is amply corroborated.

While Blair was a child in arms there was no indication that he could hear; in fact, there was every indication that he could not. I have reference, now, to the first few months after his birth. When he was about six months old his mother made the astonishing discovery that she could awaken him by speaking very gently just above his head.

From that time on, his hearing began to improve noticeably until finally he could hear the sound of one's voice, although he made no attempt to talk until he was past two years of age. About that time I discovered he could hear much better when I placed my lips against the side of his head when I spoke.

Acting on this lead, I began to practice talking to him with my lips touching his head. Remember, this was long before the modern use of bone conduction which is now employed so effectively by the manufacturers of hearing aids.

One day I noticed that Blair seemed almost hypnotized by the sound of the Victrola, so I picked him up and placed his head against the sounding board. This caused him to let out a series of gurgling sounds which resembled an attempt to laugh. After that I equipped the Victrola so he could reach it, and he soon learned to operate the machine himself. He was so fascinated that he often stood by it and played one selection after another for hours at a time.

Meanwhile, Blair was under the constant attention and observation of a noted ear specialist in Chicago, who expressed amazement at the child's ability to hear at all. This case was so puzzling that the doctor called in a group of the best-known ear specialists and, between them, they took many types of X-ray pictures of the child's skull, in their endeavor to unravel the secret of his hearing.

These examinations were continued at intervals of every few months, until Blair reached the age of nine. Then the doctor operated on one side of the child's head, for the purpose of learning what, if anything, in the way of hearing equipment, was under the skin. We learned then, for the first time, that there was no opening in the skull for the canal, and not any sign of ear equipment.

This discovery made the case more of a puzzle than ever. Nothing like it had ever been known in the annals of medical science. There had been other cases of children born without ears, but none of them had developed hearing ability. This was the feature of the case which had, and still has, the doctors puzzled. After an X-ray examination of Blair's skull, made by another noted ear specialist, from New York City, he reported to me: "Theoretically Blair has no right to hear a sound, yet he actually hears some sounds of such a high rate of vibration that you and I cannot hear them."

Generally speaking, medical science does not recognize the power of the mind as an agency which has sufficient force to provide a means of conveying sound to the brain without the aid of some ear equipment.

But the psychologist does recognize such a power as existing in the mind. I speak of the type of psychologist who has tested his knowledge by the practical affairs of life, through the trial-and-error method; the type who recognizes that the energy which keeps the stars and planets in their proper relationship and relates every atom of matter to its associated atoms in a natural, harmonious manner can and does impart knowledge to the human brain by other than the five physical senses.

As soon as I discovered that I could make Blair hear me by touching his head with my lips, I began to experiment with him. Here, again, I feel impelled to ask the reader to observe very carefully the details of what I am about to relate, for these details, as small and seemingly commonplace as they are, carry the most important evidence of the law of the power of Faith.

Having found a way to reach Blair's brain and convey sound to him, I began, when he was about three years old, to tell him "tall stories" of what he and I were going to do when he grew to manhood.

Instead of ignoring his physical handicap (as many of his relatives believed we should), I based practically all my stories on the affliction by telling Blair the time would come, after he grew up, when the lack of ears would be his greatest asset!

Frankly, I did not know, at that time, just how this promise was going to be fulfilled, but something plainly urged me to go on with the building of Blair's world of make-believe, and so I did. My desire to help Blair convert this physical handicap into an advantage was so great that I felt assured I would find some practical means of aiding him in doing so. Thus, we see there is a definite relationship between strong desire and Faith.

For example, I told Blair that when he became old enough to sell papers he could sell more papers than other boys because people would go out of their way to patronize him, seeing, as they would, that he had the courage to sell papers despite his lack of ears. Perhaps I had sufficient knowledge, in my subconscious mind, as to how Blair could convert his handicap into an advantage, to induce the Faith I had in that reality.

How prophetic a truth that promise was! Long before he was old enough to take a paper route, Blair began to request the privilege of doing so. His mother opposed the plan on the grounds that he would be subjected, because of his poor hearing, to the hazards of the street. I favored his ambition on the grounds that the experience would give him confidence and help him to adjust himself to life in a natural way, without developing inhibitions because of his affliction. There the matter stood.

One evening while his mother and I were at the theater, Blair slipped away from his nurse, went down the street to the shoemaker, borrowed six cents in capital, and invested it in newspapers. He soon sold his stock, reinvested, and sold more, until he had earned enough in profits to pay back the six cents and had forty-two cents in profits. When we got home, he was in bed asleep, his hands filled with pennies, nickels, and dimes!

His mother stood by the bed and cried when she saw him. I stood by the bed and laughed. The difference in what we saw was this: His mother saw a poor little afflicted boy who had been subjected to the dangers of the street while trying to earn money he did not need. I saw a brave little businessman who was beginning to demonstrate the truth of the things I had been telling him about his affliction becoming an asset instead of a liability. I also saw the fulfillment of the promise of Faith on which I had so adamantly relied.

Blair was five years old when he began selling papers. Already he had accepted the belief that his affliction was no handicap, and had begun to demonstrate this truth because he sold more papers than any boy on the street. Later he took the agency for the *Saturday Evening Post* and led the sales of the entire force of boys in his territory. He had more enthusiasm, initiative, and imagination than the majority of adults ever develop.

When he wanted anything, such as a bicycle or an electric train, he never asked us to give it to him; instead, he asked for the privilege of earning the money to buy whatever he wanted. On one occasion he wanted an electric train that cost more than we believed he should spend for it, so Blair took the matter out of our hands by canvassing all the neighbors and selling his services. He cleaned the snow from the walks to provide the money needed. Blair was able to compete with other children who had normal hearing, and he actually excelled most of them in all matters of importance.

Just after the doctor operated on Blair's head and discovered that he had no hearing equipment, Blair was nine years of age. My work of research in the organization of the Law of Success philosophy then made it necessary for me to travel throughout the country. Blair's mother took him to her hometown, in West Virginia, where he completed the public school, after which he entered the University of West Virginia. My influence over him ceased, therefore, at about the age of nine.

Despite the fact that he had developed only about sixty percent of his normal hearing, Blair went through the graded schools, high school, and four years of college, making grades as high as the best of his classmates who possessed normal hearing. He had not been taught lip reading, nor had he been permitted to see such a thing as sign language.

During the time I had the responsibility of influencing Blair's mind, I never permitted him to attend the schools for underprivileged children, and carefully kept him away from all reminders that his affliction was an insurmountable handicap.

My purpose was deliberate because I did not want him to develop inferiority complexes, or the feeling that he could not accomplish whatever I told him he could.

Every year, until Blair was nine, I had difficulty in getting the school authorities to allow him to enter the regular classes, because his presence made it necessary for the teachers to show him extra consideration by placing him in the front seats, and by special attention in his classes. On one such occasion I came to a deadlock with the school authorities. Accordingly, I placed Blair in a private school rather than permit the school authorities to send him to a school for underprivileged children.

These details may seem commonplace, but they are rich with meaning. They indicate how definitely I made up my mind not to accept Blair's affliction as being without a remedy. I was determined that he should pick up my state of mind and act upon it as his own!

Quite without full knowledge of the real significance and far-reaching effects of all I was doing, I was actually building the pattern, or blueprint, or impulse of thought—call it whatever you will—which was to take over, and did take over and translate into its equivalent benefit, the handicap with which Blair was born.

Keep in mind the fact that my path and Blair's seldom crossed, except for an occasional visit, from the time he was nine until he finished college and was ready for me to cooperate with him directly again. This time I was able to make good on the promise I had made during his early childhood that I would somehow see that he got his opportunity in life after he finished school and was ready for it.

That promise, as I learned afterward, was always present in his mind while he was going through school; it was doubly present in my mind. I never for one moment doubted that one day I would find a place for Blair, where he would be of great service to the world and at the same time become self-determining, despite his affliction.

In 1936 Blair finished his work at the university. Strangely, but not more so than the other parts of this life drama of which Blair was a part, about three weeks before completing his work at the university he came across a mechanical hearing aid of the bone construction type, and discovered that it supplied the extra hearing capacity he needed to give him the equivalent of normal hearing. For the first time in his life he was able to hear all that his instructors said in class.

Apparently his discovery of this hearing aid was the result of chance. The entire story cannot be dismissed as due to that cause. The law of chance seldom operates so favorably to an individual that it saves him from being a deaf-mute and helps him to convert his affliction into his greatest asset. More often the law of chance apparently works in the opposite direction, by undermining every opportunity of success because of some misfortune or physical handicap.

Blair was so elated over his "find" that he wrote me about it. Meanwhile he had dispatched a letter to the manufacturer of the hearing aid, informing him of the discovery. I answered his letter immediately, requesting him to come on to New York prepared to remain, for I saw clearly that the big opportunity through which Blair could convert his handicap into an asset was at hand.

When Blair arrived in New York, I was busily engaged at work on the manuscript of a book. I dropped all work on the book and placed my combined resources of experience and knowledge back of Blair. Within a few weeks we had planned his entire line of procedure, mapped it, and placed it on paper so it could be easily presented to others. He then took the plan to the hearing aid manufacturer and with it sold himself to the company at a starting salary of $2,600 a year and traveling expenses.

If there was ever a natural "find" of great value to a corporation, that find was made by the company that employed Blair. They readily recognized and acknowledged this fact, because they had found in Blair a "hard of hearing" case unparalleled anywhere in the world, and he had proved that the instrument had helped to correct a portion of the deficiency in that case. Other manufacturers of hearing aids became aware of Blair's presence in New York and were intent upon employing him.

While I was preparing Blair to accept his position, he lived with me and I had ample opportunity to analyze and study him at close range. This privilege proved to be a blessing. It resulted in my tearing up the manuscript on which I was working and rewriting the book for the purpose of including in it some of the important truths reflected by the present generation.

Blair began his new position, and I began studying in him a typical individual product of our modern educational system and family life. It is my belief that no young man ever came out of college, at any time or anywhere, and went directly into such an appropriate and promising position as the one Blair entered.

His employer was highly elated because he had found in Blair a marvelous subject for laboratory tests through whom the hearing aid could be tested and greatly improved, to say nothing of having found a person whose case was so positively unique that it claimed the attention of medical experts, specialists, and technicians in the hearing aid field.

The company was so pleased with the purchase of Blair's services that it began at once to send him to various places to speak before gatherings. The company's publicity experts began to write stories about his case, which commanded free publicity almost everywhere it was given out.

To make a long story short, the world of make-believe I had created for Blair had begun to come true. The experience reminded me, somewhat, of an oil promoter who "salted" a Texas farm with crude oil and sold it for what seemed to be a fabulous sum, on the representation that it contained oil, only to see the "sucker" who bought it bring in a large oil well.

I had discharged my obligation to Blair, but in doing so I had made a discovery of such enduring importance that I felt it necessary to rewrite the book on which I was working so I might include a part of my discovery.

My motive in helping my son to minimize the disadvantages of his physical affliction was that of paternal love, but the continuous and ardent application of Faith which I put into the task led me at long last into an understanding of the natural law that holds together the two opposing forces of the electron; keeps the stars and planets in their proper relationship to, and the proper distance from, one another; weaves together the personalities of people in a spirit of harmony or antagonism, according to the states of mind of the individuals;

maintains the seasons; and causes every living thing on earth to re-produce its kind; to say nothing of performing other equally important duties.

Right now, however, we are interested in the method by which one may transmute one's thoughts into their physical equivalent and determine the manner in which people relate themselves to one another, for it is in these relationships that we determine our own destinies of success or failure.

Dr. Henry C. Link alleges: "Our educational system has concentrated on mental development and has failed to give any understanding of the way emotional and personality habits are acquired or corrected."

Everyone knows that practically everything we do, from the time we begin to walk until death, is the result of habit; walking and talking are habits; our manner of eating and drinking is a habit; our sex activities are the results of habit; our relationship to other people, whether one of harmony or antagonism, is the result of habit; but no one has yet discovered why we form habits.

With a limited store of specialized knowledge of a scientific character, Henry Ford made a great success in creating a fortune and building a great industrial empire.

Mr. Ford succeeded by developing definite success habits. As far as the knowledge represented by scientific training is concerned, he has a staff of trained experts on his payrolls. From these employees he acquires the specific knowledge which he needs in practical affairs.

Most people know just as little of the causes of financial success as they know of the manner in which people acquire habits.

We know that Andrew Carnegie, with only a smattering of schooling, accumulated a fortune of more than four hundred million dollars, but what most men do not know is the exact manner in which a man with so little education was able to accumulate such a large fortune.

It is just now becoming obvious that the Carnegie fortune was the inevitable result of the self-developed and self-imposed habits of Mr. Carnegie. This great financial achievement was due perhaps more to this discipline than to the efforts of the members of his "Master Mind" to whom he gave credit for the accumulation of his money, for after all it was the Carnegie "mental attitude" (created by the dominating Carnegie thought habits) which was maintained by the members of his Master Mind and made to serve as a pattern for the guidance of their efforts.

In substance, Emerson said, "Every business is the extended shadow of one man." Yes, and if you get an accurate picture of the man who dominates the business, you will see clearly the maker of the habits which determine the success or the failure of the business. You will see also, if you look carefully, that the habit builder of a business who moves with definiteness of plan and purpose usually succeeds. He is the Henry Ford, the Andrew Carnegie, the Thomas Edison, the John D. Rockefeller.

"So," someone exclaims, "it is the individual after all who determines whether a business succeeds or fails, and not the automatic working of Faith or Cosmic Habit-force."

The answer is "Yes" and "No." The individual cuts the pattern of a business, through his mental attitude and his thought habits; but Faith converts that pattern into balances in red or black ink, according to the nature of the habits.

My conclusions on this subject are more than personal opinions, as I shall hope to prove later.

Knowledge is not power. As incredible as it may seem, knowledge, of itself, is not the cause of success. It required almost thirty years of research for me to prove the truth of this conclusion. I utterly overlooked the real cause of success and failure until I came into a better understanding of Faith, the force back of all habits. Faith translates them into their material counterparts of success and enables one to put knowledge to work.

Habits are inseparably related to the ego. Therefore let us leave my personal story here and turn to the analysis of this greatly misunderstood subject, in its relationship to the development of Faith.

Before we begin the analysis of ego, let us recognize that it is the medium through which Faith and all other states of mind operate.

Throughout this chapter great emphasis has been placed upon the distinction between passive Faith and active Faith. The ego is the medium of expression of all action. Therefore we must know something of its nature and possibilities. We must learn how to stimulate the ego and how to control and guide it. Above all, we must disabuse our minds of the popular error of believing the ego to be only the medium of expression of vanity. The word "ego" is of Latin origin, and it means "I." But it also means a driving force which can be organized and made to serve as the medium for translating desire into Faith through action.

THE MISUNDERSTOOD POWER OF EGO

As everyone knows, the word "ego" has reference to all the factors of one's personality. It is therefore obvious that the ego is subject to development, guidance, and control through the principle of habit.

A great philosopher who had devoted his entire life to the study of the human body and mind provided us with a practical foundation for the study of the ego when he said:

"Your body, whether living or dead, is a collection of millions of little energies that can never die.

"These energies are separate and individual; at times they act in some degree of harmony.

"The human body is a drifting mechanism of life, capable but not accustomed to control the forces within, except as habit, will, cultivation or special excitement may marshal these forces to the accomplishment of some important end.

"We are satisfied from many experiments that this power of marshalling and using these energies can be, in every person, cultivated to a high degree.

"The air, sunlight, food and water you take, are agents of a force that comes from the sky and earth. You idly float upon the tide of circumstances to make up your day's life, and the opportunities of being something better than you are drift beyond your reach and pass away.

"Humanity is hemmed in by so many influences that, from time immemorial, no real effort has been made to gain control of the impulses that run loose in the world. It has been, and still is, easier to let things do as they will rather than exert the will to direct them.

> ✳
> *Faith attracts only that which is constructive and creative. Fear attracts only that which is destructive.*

"But the dividing line between success and failure is found at the stage where aimless drifting ceases.

"We are all creatures of emotions, passions, circumstances and accident. What the mind will be, what the heart will be, what the body will be, are problems which are shaped by the drift of life, even when special attention is given to any of them.

"If you will sit down and think for a while, you will be surprised to know how much of your life has been mere drift.

"Look at any created life, and see its efforts to express itself. The tree sends its branches toward the sunlight, struggles through its leaves to inhale air; and, even underground, sends forth its roots in search of water. This you call inanimate life; but it represents a force that comes from some source and operates for some purpose.

"There is no place on the globe where energy is not found.

"The air is so loaded with it that in the cold north the sky shines in boreal rays; and wherever the frigid temperature yields to the warmth, the electric conditions may alarm man. Water is but a liquid union of gases, and is charged with electrical, mechanical and chemical energies, any one of which is capable of doing great service and great damage to man.

"Even ice, in its coldest phase, has energy, for it is not subdued, nor even still; its force has broken mountain rocks into fragments. This energy about us we are drinking in water, eating in food and breathing in air. Not a chemical molecule is free from it; not an atom can exist without it. We are a combination of individual energies."

Man consists of two forces, one tangible in the form of his physical body, with its myriads of individual cells, each endowed with intelligence and energy, and the other intangible, in the form of an ego—the organized dictator which may control his thoughts and deeds.

The tangible portion of a man weighing 160 pounds is composed of about fifteen chemical elements, all of which are known. They are:

95 pounds of oxygen

38 pounds of carbon

15 pounds of hydrogen

4 pounds of nitrogen

4½ pounds of calcium

6 ounces of chlorine

4 ounces of sulfur

3½ ounces of potassium

3 ounces of sodium

¼ ounce of iron

2½ ounces of fluorine

2 ounces of magnesium

1½ ounces of silicon

Small traces of arsenic

Iodine and aluminum

These tangible parts of man are worth approximately eighty cents, and may be purchased in any modern chemical plant.

Add to these fifteen chemical elements a well-developed and properly controlled ego, and they may be worth any price the owner sets upon them. The ego is a power which cannot be purchased at any price, but it can be developed and shaped to fit any desired pattern. It comes along with the few cents' worth of chemicals, at birth, and its monetary value depends upon what the owner does with it.

An Edison develops and guides his ego in the fields of creative investigation and the world finds a genius whose worth cannot be estimated in terms of dollars.

A Henry Ford guides his ego in the field of individual transportation and gives to it such stupendous value that it changes the trend of civilization by removing frontiers and converting mountain trails into public highways.

A Marconi magnetizes his ego with a keen desire to harness the ether and lives to see his wireless communication system make the whole world akin by instantaneous exchange of thought.

These men, and all others who have contributed to the march of progress, have given the world an idea of the power a well-developed ego represents. The difference between men who make valuable contributions to mankind and those who merely take up space is entirely a difference of ego, because the ego is the driving force behind all forms of action.

Liberty and freedom, the two major goals of all people, are available to every individual in exact proportion to the development and use he makes of his ego.

A brief analysis of these two desirable stations of life, liberty and freedom, will provide a better understanding of the potential power of the ego.

You have liberty when no other person restrains, retards, or controls you in any manner.

You have freedom when you do not restrain yourself, through fear or self-limitation of any nature.

Freedom is something which cannot be secured, except through the efforts of an individual, by proper development and use of his own ego.

Liberty may be acquired through the aid of others. There can be no freedom without liberty, and there can be neither freedom nor liberty except by strict control and definite guidance of one's ego.

It sometimes happens that men do not discover the real source of freedom until they lose their liberty and are forced to take introspective inventory of their own ego.

Every person who has properly related himself to his own ego has both liberty and freedom in whatever proportions he desires. A man's ego determines the manner in which he relates himself to all other people. More important still, it determines the policy under which he relates his own body and mind wherein is patterned every hope, aim, and purpose by which he establishes his destiny.

A man's ego is his greatest asset or his greatest liability, and the only thing he may build to suit his own desires.

Perhaps the most abused and misunderstood word in the English language is "ego." This word has been abused by the common practice of associating it with vanity and self-love.

Every highly successful person possesses a well-developed and self-disciplined ego, but there is a third factor associated with ego which determines its potency for good or evil—the self-control necessary to transmute its power into any desired plan or purpose.

With this brief preparation, I am now ready to explain how I arrived at the conclusion that controlled ego is at the bottom of all human achievement. In the analysis I shall reveal some of the results of thirty years of careful observation of the manner in which the mind operates, clearly indicating which of the observations are known facts, which are deductions.

As I unfold this description of the great drama in which men create their own earthly destinies, it will become clear why knowledge, education, facts, and experiences are of themselves no guarantee of success.

It will become clear, also, why some people are so long in finding the secret of successful application of the principles of achievement. This explanation will provide a guide to all who, in the future, wish to apply these principles with the object of achieving material success.

I shall emphasize one important truth which, if properly interpreted, will give a new meaning to the principles of achievement.

The truth I wish to convey is this: The starting point of all achievement is some plan by which one's ego can be made success conscious.

In other words, the person who succeeds must do so by properly developing his own ego, impressing it with the object of his desires, and removing from it all forms of limitation and dissipation.

The place to start using the principles of achievement is in the development of one's own ego. Nothing that was uncovered during my thirty years of research was more impressive or helpful than the obvious fact that every man of outstanding achievement whom I analyzed had gained control of his ego.

Autosuggestion (or self-hypnosis) is the medium by which one may attune his ego to any desired rate of vibration. Every successful person makes constant use of this principle.

Unless you catch the full significance of the principle of autosuggestion, you will miss the most important part of this chapter, because the nature of a person's ego is due entirely to the extent of his knowledge and application of self-suggestion.

Stating the matter in another way, before a person can sell the world any idea, he must first sell it to himself.

Every master salesman, no matter in what calling, understands and uses this principle. If he did not understand it, he would not be a master.

People who have what is popularly called a pleasing or charming personality are those who by chance or design have colored their own ego with definite, positive qualities.

No man can be master of anything or anyone to which his own ego is bound and fettered by fear or self-depreciation.

No man can express himself in terms of opulence while most of his energies are required in a struggle against poverty. Nevertheless, one should not lose sight of the fact that many men of great wealth began in poverty, which suggests that this and all other fears can be conquered!

There are hundreds of different parts to an automobile, every one of which is essential for the satisfactory and safe operation of the machine. These parts are so assembled and coordinated that they have been reduced to three important factors as far as the average driver is concerned, namely, (1) a steering wheel, (2) an accelerator, and (3) a set of brakes. Through these three points of contact an automobile can be put into motion, guided over any desired course, and stopped at will.

The human machine is infinitely more complicated than the automobile. It is subject to manipulation through many types of stimuli and many parts, but in the form of desires, fears, and emotions. In the final analysis all the principles of success and all the principles of failure can be consolidated and expressed through one single factor, the human ego.

The ego embodies the steering wheel, the accelerator, and the brakes with which the physical machine of an individual is started, guided, and stopped.

In the one word, ego, may be found the composite effects of all the principles of achievement, coordinated into one single unit of power which may be directed to any desired end by any individual who is the complete master of his ego.

The egotist who makes himself offensive is one who has not dis-covered how to relate himself to his ego in a manner which gives it constructive use.

Most expressions of egotism are nothing but efforts to conceal inferiority complexes. The person who fails to relate himself to his ego in a manner that gives it constructive guidance is sure to make the same mistake in his method of relating himself to other indi-viduals.

Constructive application of the ego is made through expressions of one's hopes, desires, aims, ambitions, and plans, and not by boast-fulness and self-love.

The motto of the person who is on good terms with his ego is "Deeds, not words." The desire to be great is a healthy desire, but an open expression of one's belief in his own greatness is an indication that he is not carefully building his ego, and you may be sure his proclamations of greatness are but cloaks with which to shield some fear.

THE RELATIONSHIP BETWEEN MENTAL ATTITUDE AND EGO

Understand the real nature of your ego, and you will understand the real significance of the Master Mind principle. Moreover, you will recognize the fact that to be of greatest service, the members of your Master Mind alliance must be in full sympathy with your hopes, aims, and purposes; they must not be in competition with you in any manner whatsoever. They must be willing to subordinate their own desires and personalities entirely for the attainment of your major purpose in life. They must have confidence in your integrity, and they must respect you. They must be willing to support your virtues and make allowances for your faults. They must be willing to permit you to be yourself and live your own life in your own way at all times. Lastly, they must receive from you some form of compensation which will make you as beneficial to them as they are to you.

Failure to observe the last requirement will bring an end to your Master Mind alliance, no matter who you are or with whom you are associated.

Men relate themselves to one another because of motive. There can be no permanent human relationship based upon an indefinite or vague motive. Failure to recognize this truth has cost many men the difference between penury and opulence.

One of the first and perhaps the most important secrets of Andrew Carnegie's achievements was his method of maintaining his Master Mind relationship with his business associates. He was a master at the business of selecting men for his Master Mind group who brought with them not only knowledge and intelligence, but what is more important, the ability to relate themselves to his ego according to its needs.

When a certain man heard that Mr. Carnegie had permitted Charles M. Schwab to earn as much as a million dollars in one year, he was curious to know what peculiar abilities or knowledge Mr. Schwab possessed which entitled him to receive so fabulous a sum, so he asked Mr. Carnegie to enlighten him.

"Charlie Schwab's knowledge of the steel business," said Mr. Carnegie, "may not be worth a dollar more than twenty-five thousand dollars a year, but his personality and his influence upon me are so valuable that they cannot be estimated in terms of money. His very presence gives me the courage to think in bigger terms, and the self-confidence to believe I can master all difficulties that get in my way."

A man's ego is the focal point of his being in which is centered a perfect picture of himself; a picture into which has gone every thought he has released, whether of a negative or a positive nature; a picture in which is clearly reflected all his hopes, desires, and plans; all his fears and limitations, no matter from what source they may have come.

By a careful choice of associates, with the aid of a definite purpose, a man may shape, develop, and guide his ego until it becomes an irresistible power through which he can appropriate whatever he wants of life. By neglecting to cultivate his ego, a man may drift with time and circumstance into the lowest depths of failure.

The men of great achievement are, and they always will be, those who deliberately feed, shape, and control their own egos, leaving no part of the task to chance.

So there may be no misunderstanding as to what I mean by the term "properly developed ego," I shall describe briefly the factors which enter into the development, viz.:

First, one must ally himself with one or more people who will coordinate their minds with his in a spirit of perfect harmony, for the attainment of some definite purpose, and that alliance must be continuous and active.

Moreover, it must consist of people whose spiritual and mental qualities, education, sex, and age are suited to the object of the alliance. For example, Andrew Carnegie's Master Mind group was made up of more than twenty men, each of whom brought to the alliance some quality of mind, experience, or knowledge not available through any of the others.

Second, having placed himself under the influence of the proper associates, one must adopt some definite plan by which to attain the object of his alliance and proceed to put that plan into action! If one plan proves to be inadequate, it must be supplemented or supplanted by others until one is found that will work; but there must be no change in the purpose of the alliance.

Third, one must remove one's self from the range of influence of every person and every circumstance which has even a slight tendency to cause him to feel inferior or incapable of attaining the object of his purpose. Positive egos do not grow in negative environments. On this point there can be no compromise. The line must be so clearly drawn between a man and those who exercise any form of negative influence over him that he closes the door tightly against every such person, no matter what previous ties of friendship or blood relationship may have existed between them.

Fourth, one must close the door tightly against every thought of any past experience or circumstance which tends to make him feel inferior or unhappy. Strong, vital egos cannot be developed from the all too prevalent habit of wallowing in the thoughts of unpleasant past experiences. Vital egos thrive on the hopes and desires of unattained achievements, and not upon thoughts of past failures.

Thoughts are the building blocks of which the human ego is constructed.

When the job is finished it represents, right down to the slightest shades, the exact nature of the thoughts that went into it.

It was his astonishing recognition of this fact that prompted Henry Ford to remove from his business family every person who was out of step with his business policy.

It was his complete understanding of this truth that caused Andrew Carnegie to insist upon harmony between the members of his Master Mind group and himself.

Fifth, one must surround himself with every possible physical means of impressing his mind with the nature and purpose of the ego he is developing. For example, an author should set up his workshop in a room decorated with the pictures and works of the authors in his field whom he most admires; he should fill his bookshelves with books related to his own work; he should surround himself with every possible means of conveying to his ego the exact picture he expects to express.

Sixth, the properly developed ego is at all times under the control of the individual. It must be guided to definite ends and constantly used. There must be no overinflation of the ego, in the direction of egomania by which some men destroy themselves. Egomania reflects itself in a mad desire to control others by force, examples being such men as Adolf Hitler, Benito Mussolini, and Wilhelm Hohenzollern, former Kaiser of Germany. In the development of the ego, one's motto should be "Not too much, not too little." When men begin to thirst for control over others, or to accumulate large sums of money they cannot or do not use constructively, they are treading upon dangerous ground. Power of this kind grows of its own nature and soon gets out of control.

Nature has a safety valve through which she deflates the ego and relieves the pressure of its influences when an individual goes beyond certain limits in the development of his ego. Emerson called it the law of Compensation, but whatever it is, it operates with inexorable definiteness.

Egomania drove Theodore Roosevelt to attempt a third term in the White House. When he failed, his ego was so shaken that he soon died.

Napoleon Bonaparte began to die because of a crushed ego the day he landed on St. Helena. People who retire from all forms of work, after having led active lives, generally atrophy and die very soon. If they live, they are miserably unhappy. A healthy ego is one that is always in use and under complete control.

Seventh, ego is constantly undergoing changes, for better or for worse, because of the nature of one's thoughts.

There is no adequate method of describing the exact period of time required for the transformation of a desire into its physical equivalent. The nature of the desire, the circumstances which influence it, the intensity of the desire itself—all of these are determining factors in connection with the time required for the transformation from the thought stage to the physical stage. The state of mind known as Faith is so favorable to the quick change of desire into its physical equivalent that it has been known to make the change almost instantly.

Man matures physically within about twenty years, but mentally—which means his ego—requires from thirty-five to sixty years for maturity. This fact explains why men seldom begin to accumulate material riches in great abundance until they are around fifty years of age. An ego which can acquire and retain great material wealth is, of necessity, one that has undergone self-discipline and has acquired self-confidence, Definiteness of Purpose, initiative, imagination, accuracy of judgment, and other qualities without which no ego has the power to procure and hold wealth.

A few years before the beginning of the world depression, the owner of a small beauty parlor turned over a back room in her place of business to an old man who needed a place to sleep. The man had no money, but he did have considerable knowledge of the methods of compounding cosmetics. Accordingly, the young woman who gave the old man a place to sleep provided him with an opportunity to pay for his room by compounding the cosmetics she needed in her business.

Very soon the two entered into a Master Mind alliance that was destined to bring them economic freedom. First, they entered into a business partnership with the object of compounding cosmetics to be sold from house to house, by agents, the woman providing the money for the necessary raw materials, the man doing the labor.

> *Faith influences one to look for and to expect to find the best there is in men. Fear discovers only their weaknesses.*

Their first sales were made by themselves, the woman devoting her evenings to selling from house to house, the man also devoting a portion of each day to selling.

After a few years the Master Mind arrangement between the two had proved so advantageous, they decided to solidify it by marriage.

The old man had been in the cosmetics business for the better portion of his adult life, but had not achieved success. The young woman had barely made a living operating a beauty parlor. The happy combination of the two brought them into possession of power neither had known prior to their alliance, and they began to succeed financially almost from the very first day of their business alliance.

At the beginning of the business depression they were compounding cosmetics in one small room, and selling their products personally from door to door. By the end of the depression they had grown to where they were compounding their cosmetics in a large factory with over a hundred employees working steadily, and more than four thousand salespeople selling their products throughout the country.

During the first ten years of their alliance they accumulated a fortune of two million dollars, despite the fact that they were operating during depression years, when such luxuries as cosmetics were naturally difficult to sell.

They have placed themselves beyond the need for money for the remainder of their lives. Moreover, they have gained financial freedom on precisely the same knowledge and the same opportunities they possessed prior to their Master Mind alliance, when both were poverty-stricken.

Interested in knowing the secret by which two practically unknown people of mediocre ability and little education achieved the miracle of legitimately accumulating a fortune during the days of uncertainty, I traveled halfway across the continent and became their houseguest while I studied every detail of their business policies and every characteristic of personality of each of them.

These circumstances under which I was privileged to analyze these people were such that I came back with the entire story, just as it had been lived. What a significant story it is! I wish the names of these two interesting people could be mentioned, but personal consideration prevents me from revealing their names.

The motive which brought about the alliance of these two people, in their business and their marriage, was definitely economic in nature. The man is now seventy-five years of age; the woman is forty. She had previously been married to a man who failed to earn a living for her and deserted her when their child was an infant.

My observation of these people, at close range, permits me to say there is not, and never has been, the slightest feeling between the two which even remotely resembles love. However, there is harmony between them. This is a significant fact in view of the great emphasis that Andrew Carnegie placed upon harmony as an essential in the successful operation of the Master Mind.

On the back of the lot on which their house is situated they have an elaborate swimming pool which no one but the "lord and master" is permitted to use except on very rare occasions, on invitation from him.

The house is elaborately furnished, but no one—not even invited guests—is permitted to take a turn at the piano or sit in one of the chairs in the living room without special invitation.

The main dining room is equipped with ornate furniture, with a long dining table suitable for use on "state" occasions, but the family and guests are seldom permitted to use it. They dine in the breakfast room.

A gardener is constantly at work on the lawn, but no one is permitted to cut a flower without special invitation from the man of the house.

Nothing can be served at the table which the head of the house does not personally like.

Such conversation as is carried on is conducted entirely by the head of the house. His wife never speaks unless she is definitely requested to do so, and then her speech is brief and carefully weighed so as not to irritate her "master."

Their business is incorporated, and the man is president of the corporation. He has an elaborate office furnished with a large hand-carved desk and overstuffed chairs.

On the wall directly in front of the desk is an enormous painting of himself, at which he gazes with obvious admiration almost constantly.

When speaking of the business, and particularly of the unusual success it has enjoyed during the country's worst depression, the man takes full credit for all that has been accomplished; so much so, in fact, that he never even mentions his wife's name in connection with the business.

While the wife goes to the business daily, she has no office and no desk. She is apt to be found strolling around the factory, as nonchalantly as if she were an outside visitor.

The man's name is on every package of merchandise that leaves the factory. It is painted in large letters on every delivery truck they operate, and it appears in large type on every piece of sales literature and every advertisement they publish. Her name is conspicuous by its absence.

The man believes he built the business, that he runs it, that it could not operate without him. The truth of the matter is precisely the opposite. His ego built the business, and runs it, and the business might continue to run just as well or better without him, for the very good reason that his wife developed that ego and she could do the same for any other man under similar circumstances.

Patiently, with purpose aforethought and self-control, this man's wife completely submerged her own personality into that of her husband, and step by step fed his ego the sort of food that removed from it every trace of inferiority, wiped out a poverty complex born of a lifetime of deprivation, and hypnotized her husband into believing himself to be the moving spirit of the business.

In truth every business policy, every business move, and every forward step the business has taken is the result of her ideas so cleverly placed in his mind that he fails to recognize their source. In reality she is the entire brains of the business, he the mere window dressing; but the combination is unbeatable, evidence of which may be found in their astounding financial achievement.

The manner in which this woman effaced herself was not only evidence of her perfect self-control, but it was evidence of her wisdom, for she probably could not have accomplished the same results by any other method.

If these two persons should allow anything to break the spirit of harmony in which they now work, both would probably fall more rapidly than they have ever risen. Their power apparently consists entirely of the synthetic ego this clever woman has developed in her husband. The ego will live only as long as she carefully protects and stimulates it.

Without her constant influence, the old man would become exactly what he was before she allied herself with him—a pitiful failure. I make this statement in the most impersonal manner, but it is correct.

Here, then, is evidence that the major difference between poverty and riches is merely the difference between an ego that is dominated by an inferiority complex and one that is dominated by a feeling of superiority. This old man would have died a homeless pauper if a clever woman had not blended her mind with his in such a way as to feed his ego on thoughts of opulence.

This is a fact from which there is no escape. Moreover, this case is only one of many. The only difference is that in this case all the facts for the analysis were easily available, while in the majority of cases the facts are cleverly hidden.

For a great many years after my first meeting with Henry Ford, I was baffled by the source of Mr. Ford's stupendous ability to surmount difficulties. Then quite by chance I met a close neighbor of the Fords who gave me a confidential report of the relationship between Mr. and Mrs. Ford.

The Fords began to apply the Master Mind principle as the basis of their personal relationship from the very beginning, although Mrs. Ford has always so completely submerged her own personality that the public rarely sees her name in print.

I am reliably informed that back in the early days, when Ford lacked money with which to carry on experiments in connection with his horseless buggy, Mrs. Ford influenced him to spend their last cent for that purpose.

I am also reliably informed that Mr. Ford never makes an important business decision without first talking it over with his wife. The Ford ego—famous because of what people do not know about it—is a combination of his own and that of his wife. The definiteness and singleness of purpose, persistence, self-reliance, and self-control— so obviously parts of the Ford ego—can be traced to Mrs. Ford's influence.

The Ford ego, quite unlike that of the cosmetician just described, functions without glamour. There are no large pictures of Henry Ford in his office, but make no mistake about this: Mr. Ford's influence is felt by every person associated directly or indirectly with his vast empire, and something of Henry Ford himself goes into every automobile that leaves his factory. These are the means whereby he expresses his ego: through mechanical perfection; through transportation service at a popular price; through the employment of a large army of men and women.

Mr. Ford is not above appreciating a word of praise, but he has never gone out of his way to attract it. His ego does not require constant pampering such as that given the cosmetician by his wife.

Mr. Ford's method of appropriating the knowledge and experience of other men is entirely different from that of Andrew Carnegie, and most other business magnates. His ego is so modest and unassuming that he neither encourages favorable comment upon his work nor goes out of his way to express any form of appreciation of compliments.

Henry Ford has one of the truly great minds of the world. He is great because he has learned how to recognize the laws of nature and adapt himself to them in a manner beneficial to himself; but I believe that his greatness is derived in part from his association with his wife and other great minds, including those of Edison, Burbank, Burroughs, and Firestone, with whom he had a friendly alliance that extended over a long period of years. Every year for a great number of years these five men left their respective businesses and went away together to some quiet, out-of-the-way spot, where they exchanged thoughts and fed their egos on the food each craved.

Henry Ford's personality, his business policies, and even the general appearance of his automobiles began to show a decided improvement from year to year, because of his association with these men. Their influence upon him was definite, deep, and profound.

I have observed, by studying men of achievement, the interesting fact that the space a man occupies in the world through his influence is in exact proportion to the extent that he dominates his own ego. The cosmetician whom I have mentioned occupies and controls only the space bounded by his own household and the factory in which his employees compound cosmetics.

Henry Ford occupies in one way or another practically all of the space of the world, and influences the trend of civilization. Because he is the master of his ego, Ford is capable of acquiring practically every material thing on earth he desires; in fact, he has already done so.

The cosmetician expresses his ego in many forms of petty selfishness; consequently, he has limited his influence to the mere accumulation of money and the domination (without their willing consent) of a few people including his own household and business organization.

Ford expresses his ego in ever expanding and increasing terms of benefit to mankind and, without making a bid for it, finds himself an influencing factor throughout the civilized world.

This is an astounding thought! It offers vitally important suggestions as to the type of ego one should endeavor to create.

Thirty years of almost continuous research has led to the inevitable conclusion that the only important difference between people is the variance of their egos.

Henry Ford has developed an ego which extends itself into plans that belt the earth. He thinks in terms of the manufacture and distribution of automobiles.

He thinks in terms of thousands of men working for him.

He thinks in terms of millions of dollars of working capital.

He thinks in terms of a business he dominates by establishing his own policy for procuring working capital.

He thinks in terms of keeping his business out of the hands of others by setting up pay schedules and working conditions far more favorable than any of his workers could reasonably demand.

He thinks in terms of economy through efficient coordination of the effort of the thousands of men who work for him.

He thinks in terms of harmonious cooperation between himself and his business associates, and puts his thoughts into action by removing from his organization any man who does not see eye to eye with him.

These are the qualities which nourish, feed, and maintain the irrepressible Ford ego. There is nothing difficult to understand about any of these qualities. They are qualities which any man may have by simply adopting and using them.

Turn the spotlight on any one of the many men who have begun building automobiles since Henry Ford started; study that man carefully and you will learn quickly why one remembers few of the men or what automobiles they temporarily produced.

You will discover that every one of Ford's competitors who fell by the wayside did so because of self-imposed limitations or dissipation of the ego.

You will also find that practically every one of those forgotten men apparently possessed as much intelligence as Ford. The majority of them not only had better schooling than he, but they also had more dynamic personalities.

The major difference between Ford and his competitors is this:

He developed an ego that extended itself far beyond his personal achievements; the others so limited their egos that they soon caught up with them, and their plans went on the rocks for the want of that something which an extended ego does to lead a man onward.

Among the hundreds of Ford competitors who started soon after he began, there was one who made such rapid progress that he would have eclipsed Ford's achievements in the industry, if something had not gone wrong with his ego.

His outstanding features were (1) a magnetic personality with the attracting power of a Franklin D. Roosevelt; (2) a well-rounded education; (3) marvelous capacity as a salesman, with ability to induce men to coordinate their efforts in a spirit of harmony; and (4) a record of achievement in business of sufficient magnitude to enable him to procure all the working capital he needed.

When he was at the height of his career, he was the head of his own company, manufacturing an automobile which led the field in its price class.

He had before him a future far brighter than any Ford enjoyed at the outset of his business. His name was then a national byword.

His ego was dynamic, powerful, and ambitious. According to the rules by which we usually measure men, he should have outdistanced Ford. But something happened to him at the very height of his career which sent him sprawling into oblivion and quickly erased his name from the list of automobile producers. The thing that happened was this: Success went to his head and he allowed his ego to become so greatly inflated that it literally blew up and burst.

The well-balanced ego is not subject to serious influence by either commendation or condemnation.

Men who succeed in their chosen calling always establish a definite goal, lay plans for the attainment of that goal, and move toward its attainment by the straightest and shortest possible route, never stopping to listen to their enemies nor spending too much time with friends. In other words, the successful man controls his own ego against overindulgence in, or influence by, the things he likes most, as well as the things he likes least.

I can safely say that of the hundreds of men I have known who attained high positions in life only to wind up poverty-stricken and miserable, the majority of them failed because someone influenced them to form the habit of drifting.

No one ever heard of Ford spending an evening among social butterflies and cocktail glasses. No one ever read a newspaper account of Ford having boasted of his achievements. The Ford ego was not evolved from such influences, and that is why he is healthy, hale, and rich at an age when most men consider themselves ready for the scrap heap.

The Ford ego is exactly as Mr. Ford wants it. He is in control of his ego at all times, therefore he occupies more space and extends more influence in the world than fifty percent of the people now living. What an astounding fact!

Ford's power is not based upon knowledge alone. It is not based upon intelligence alone. It is not based upon education. It is in no way associated with luck, good fortune, or his having been born under the right star. The Ford power is nothing but the expression of the self-made Ford ego that is absolutely free from all manner of fear and is not fettered by any self-imposed limitations.

When Ford told a group of newspapermen he had come to Washington, at President Roosevelt's invitation, "to let the President see a man who did not want anything," he was neither egotistical nor facetious. He spoke the truth. Ford can get any material thing on earth he wishes, or its equivalent, because Ford has developed and continues to control his own ego. There is no other mystery to his great power.

Mr. Ford has in his organization thousands of men better educated than he, with more personality than he, and with as much intelligence as he. The major difference between him and them is solely a difference in ego. He has a self-made ego free of limitation and dissipation. The others have egos which have grown out of their drifting attitude, their lack of Definiteness of Purpose, and their limitation of ambition. There is no other difference, and it is a difference which distinguishes success from failure in every walk of life.

The Ford ego has now become so definitely permanent that I doubt if Ford himself could change it. That ego is so positive that it does not recognize such things as immovable obstacles. This habitual attitude has conditioned Mr. Ford's mind perfectly for the continuous operation of Faith. It knows nothing about retreating; it moves only in one direction and that is forward.

The human ego—the personality of the individual—may be likened to a magnet which attracts everything that harmonizes with its nature. Ford magnetizes his ego with desires and plans that have practically no limitations. He thereby commandeers into his service Faith, the most powerful law of nature, with which the physical counterpart of his desires is acquired.

Henry Ford's ego is literally absorbed by a single obsession to the realization of which he subordinates all other desires.

Any man who can focus his desires upon a single definite purpose and then fan that desire into a white flame of obsession can have the object of that desire as easily as Ford built his vast industrial empire, which, as everyone knows, is and has for many years been his obsession.

The great leaders are known to have attained their greatness as the result of some outside influence which enabled them to remove limitations from their ego and replace them with Faith.

Without doubt Napoleon Bonaparte's astounding ego was controlled by the influence of his first wife. When he voluntarily removed himself from that influence, his permanent failure was not far away.

Charles Dickens wrote his greatest book, *David Copperfield*, as the result of the change in his ego brought about by the influence of his first sweetheart, and incidentally, he wrote that book around his own experiences.

Lincoln would doubtlessly have remained an obscure lawyer if his love for Anne Rutledge had not awakened his ego and magnetized it with her ambition.

The second Mrs. Thomas A. Edison was the urge back of the famous Edison ego which gave America a great inventive genius. From the first time he ever saw her until his death she was the moving spirit of his life. The changes she made in his ego were lasting and profound. I have Edison's word for this.

These are some of the men of outstanding achievement whose egos were modified by the women of their choice. I have observed hundreds of men of lesser achievements whose success was due to the influence of their wives.

Every man comes finally to resemble those who make the strongest impression upon his mind.

We are all creatures of imitation, and naturally we try to imitate the heroes of our choice. Fortunate, indeed, is the person whose hero is a person of great Faith, because hero worship carries with it something of the nature of the one who is worshipped.

In conclusion, let me summarize what has been said on the subject of ego by calling attention to the fact that it represents the fertile garden spot wherein one may develop all the stimuli that inspire active Faith, or by neglecting to do so one may allow this fertile soil to produce a negative crop of fear and doubt and indecision leading to failure. Applied Faith, so critical to taking action necessary for success, is inspired, commanded, and propelled by the ego.

FAITH UNMISTAKABLY IDENTIFIES ITSELF THROUGH THE LOOK IN ONE'S EYES, THE EXPRESSION ON THE FACE, AND THE TONE OF THE VOICE.

FEAR IDENTIFIES ITSELF THROUGH THE SAME SOURCES.

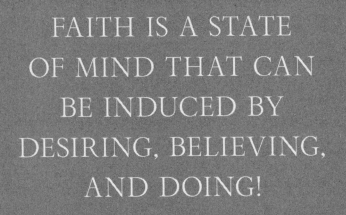

FAITH IS A STATE
OF MIND THAT CAN
BE INDUCED BY
DESIRING, BELIEVING,
AND DOING!

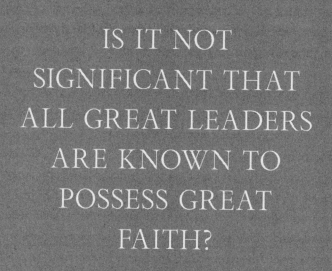

IS IT NOT
SIGNIFICANT THAT
ALL GREAT LEADERS
ARE KNOWN TO
POSSESS GREAT
FAITH?

❊

PEOPLE DO NOT LACK STRENGTH; THEY LACK WILL.

—VICTOR HUGO

✳

CHAPTER TWO

ENTHUSIASM

Enthusiasm—the emotions put into action through spiritual power—is the beginning of all great achievements of whatever nature!

Everyone desires to achieve personal success, in one form or another, but only those who acquire the habit of fanning the fire of enthusiasm into a white heat of obsessional desire ever attain noteworthy success.

More than forty years ago the stepmother of a young mountaineer called him into the family living room, excluded the other children of the family from the conference, and said something which changed his entire life for the better, and at the same time planted in his mind a desire which he has transplanted into thousands of other minds—the desire to become self-determining through the rendering of useful service.

This boy was only eleven years of age, but he was known among the mountain folk as "the worst boy in the county"! This is what his stepmother said to him:

People misjudge you. They call you the worst boy in the county, but you are not the worst boy; you are the most active boy, and all you need is a definite purpose to which you can direct the attention of your enquiring mind. You have a keen imagination and plenty of ini- tiative. Therefore I suggest that you become a writer. If you will do this, and give as much interest to reading and writing as you have been devoting to playing pranks on the neighbors, you may live to see the time when your influence will be felt throughout this state.

There was something in the stepmother's tone of voice which registered effectively in the "bad" boy's mind. He caught the spirit of enthusiasm in which his stepmother had spoken to him, and began, immediately, to act on her suggestion.

By the time he was fifteen years of age he was writing newspaper and magazine stories that were being published in small newspapers and magazines. His writing was not brilliant, but it carried a spirit of enthusiasm which made it readable.

At the age of twenty-five he was assigned, by the editor of *Bob Tay- lor's Magazine*, to write the story of Andrew Carnegie's achievements in industry. That assignment was destined to bring another change in his life, for it led not only to an opportunity to write books that would make his influence felt throughout the state, as his stepmother had sug- gested, but that influence now extends throughout a major portion of the world, and it is obviously destined to render useful service in helping to save the American way of life from annihilation.

In the interview with Andrew Carnegie, this young writer was moved by Mr. Carnegie's enthusiasm. He acquired the spirit of that enthusiasm, and it has been that spirit which has made his books "best sellers" for many years.

I am proud to state that I am that "bad boy."

This chapter on enthusiasm begins in the private study of Andrew

Carnegie, during our 1908 meeting, where he is coaching his new protégé in the art of controlled enthusiasm!

HILL:

> I am ready, Mr. Carnegie, for your analysis of the principle of individual achievement which I believe you call enthusiasm. I wish you to define the meaning of this term and describe how one may develop enthusiasm at will.

CARNEGIE:

> Enthusiasm can be developed by stimulating the faculty of the emotions.

HILL:

> Then enthusiasm is emotion in action?

CARNEGIE:

> That is the brief way of stating it. Perhaps it would be more correctly stated if one said that enthusiasm is voluntary emotion— a feeling that one initiates at will. But you have overlooked one very important factor in your question, the question of control of enthusiasm. It is just as important to know how to modify, control, or shut off entirely the action of the emotions as it is to know how to start them into action.
>
> Before we go into the discussion of emotional control, however, let us take inventory of the benefits available through enthusiasm. To begin with, let us be reminded that enthusiasm is the result of desire, expressed in terms of action, and based upon motive. No normal person ever goes into a heat of enthusiasm without a motive. It is obvious, therefore, that the beginning of all enthusiasm is desire based on motive.

There are two types of enthusiasm, passive and active. Perhaps it would be more accurate if I said that enthusiasm may be expressed in two ways: passively, through the stimulation of emotional feeling, and actively, by the expression of feeling, through words or deeds.

HILL:

Which is the more beneficial of the two—the active expression or the passive?

CARNEGIE:

The answer to that depends upon the circumstances. Of course passive enthusiasm always precedes the expression of active enthusiasm, as one must feel it before he can express it in any form of action or words.

There are times when the expression of enthusiasm may be detrimental to one's interest, as it may indicate overeagerness, or disclose one's state of mind under circumstances when he does not wish to have it known to others. It is highly important, then, that one learn how to withhold the expression of his feelings under all circumstances. It is also important that one acquire the ability to give open expression of his feelings at will. In both instances, the control is the important factor.

Now let us briefly describe some of the benefits of both passive and active enthusiasm. First of all, let us remember that enthusiasm (which may be an expression of one or more of the emotions) stimulates the vibration of thought and makes it more intense, thus starting the faculty of the imagination to work in connection with the motive which inspired the enthusiasm.

Enthusiasm gives tone quality to one's voice and makes it pleasing and impressive. A salesman or public speaker would be ineffective without the ability to turn on his enthusiasm at will. The same is true of one who engages in ordinary conversation. Even the most prosaic subjects can be made interesting if they are expressed with enthusiasm. Without it the most interesting subjects can be boresome.

Enthusiasm inspires initiative, both in thought and in physical action. It is very difficult for one to do well that in which he has no feeling of enthusiasm.

Enthusiasm dispels physical fatigue and overcomes laziness. It has been said that there are no lazy men. What appears to be a lazy man is one who is moved by no motive over which he becomes enthusiastic.

Enthusiasm stimulates the entire nervous system and causes it to perform its duties more efficiently, including, in particular, the function of digestion of food. For this reason the meal hour should be the pleasantest hour of the day, and it should never become the occasion for settling personal or family differences of opinion, nor should it become the time for the correction of the faults of children.

Enthusiasm stimulates the subconscious section of the brain and puts it to work in connection with the motive which inspires enthusiasm. In fact, there is no known method of stimulating the subconscious mind voluntarily except that of inspired feeling. Here let us emphasize the fact that the subconscious mind acts upon all feeling, whether it is negative or positive. It will act on the emotion of fear as quickly as it will act on the emotion of love. Or, it will go to work on the worry over poverty as quickly as it will act on the feeling of opulence. It is important, therefore, to recognize that enthusiasm is the positive expression of feeling.

Enthusiasm is contagious. It affects everyone within its range, a fact that is well known to all master salesmen. Moreover, one may influence others through either the active or the passive expression of enthusiasm.

Enthusiasm discourages all forms of negative thought, and dispels fear and worry, thus preparing the mind for the expression of Faith.

Enthusiasm is the twin brother of the faculty of the will, it being the major source of sustained action of the will! It is also a sustaining force in connection with persistence. We might say, therefore, that willpower, persistence, and enthusiasm are triplets which give one sustained action with a minimum loss of physical energy. As a matter of fact, enthusiasm converts fatigue and static energy into active energy.

Emerson spoke a deeper truth than most people recognize when he said that "nothing great was ever achieved without enthusiasm." He must have known that enthusiasm gives quality to every word a man speaks, to every task at which he sets his hands.

HILL:

I have heard it said that writers unconsciously project their enthusiasm or the lack of it in every word they write, so that even the casual reader may interpret the writer's mental attitude as he wrote. Is this a sound theory?

CARNEGIE:

Not just a sound theory, but a fact. Try it out on yourself and be convinced. A man's writing may be translated into other languages, but it will very largely carry with it the same tempo of enthusiasm the writer felt when writing. I have heard it said that the writer of advertisements who feels no enthusiasm in connection with his copy writes poor copy, no matter how many facts he may describe. I have also heard it said that the lawyer who feels no enthusiasm over his case fails to be convincing to judges and juries. And there is plenty of evidence that the enthusiasm of a doctor is his greatest remedy in the sickroom. Enthusiasm is one of the greatest builders of confidence, for everyone knows that enthusiasm and Faith are closely related.

Enthusiasm connotes hope and courage and belief in one's self. I do not recall ever having promoted a man to a higher position, or ever having employed a man for a responsible position, who did not first demonstrate his enthusiasm over the possibilities of the position. I have observed that the young people who have gone to work in our offices, as clerks and stenographers, have promoted themselves into more responsible positions in almost exact ratio to the enthusiasm they displayed in their work.

HILL:

Is it not possible for one to display too much enthusiasm for his own good?

CARNEGIE:

Yes, uncontrolled enthusiasm often is as detrimental as no enthusiasm. For example, the man who is so enthusiastic over himself and his own ideas that he monopolizes the conversation when conversing with others is sure to be unpopular, not to mention the fact that he misses many opportunities to learn by listening to others.

Then, there is the man who becomes too enthusiastic over the roulette wheel or the horses, and the man who becomes more enthusiastic over ways and means of getting something for nothing than he does over rendering useful service, not to mention the woman who becomes more enthusiastic over card parties and society than she does over making her home and herself attractive to her husband. This sort of uncontrolled enthusiasm may be very detrimental to all whom it affects.

HILL:

Is enthusiasm of any value to the man engaged in manual labor?

CARNEGIE:

Well, I can best answer that by calling your attention to the fact that most of the higher officials of my own organization began in the humblest of positions. The man who made the greatest progress of all my associates began as a stake driver, and he formerly worked as a teamster. His boundless enthusiasm was the quality that first attracted my attention to him, and it was this same quality that lifted him, step by step, into the highest position we had to offer.

Yes, enthusiasm can be of value to anyone, regardless of his occupation, for it is a quality that attracts friends, establishes confidence, and breaks down the opposition of others.

HILL:

What part, if any, does enthusiasm or lack of it play in the relationship of the home?

CARNEGIE:

Well, let us go back a little way, and consider the part that enthusiasm plays in bringing men and women together in a bond of marriage. Did you ever hear of a man winning the woman of his choice without displaying considerable enthusiasm over her? And it also works the other way around. A man will not be inclined to propose marriage to the woman who shows no enthusiasm over him.

Mutual enthusiasm, therefore, is usually the basis of marriage, and woe unto the party to the marriage who allows that enthusiasm to wane afterward. We speak of the relationship as love, but what is love but mutual enthusiasm of two people over each other?

HILL:

Under what circumstances does enthusiasm reach its highest degree of personal benefit?

CARNEGIE:

In a Master Mind alliance, two or more people work together, in a spirit of perfect harmony, for the attainment of a definite purpose. Here the enthusiasm of each member of the alliance projects itself into the mind of all the other members, and the sum total of enthusiasm thus created, by the harmonious blending of a group of minds, becomes available to and influences each individual.

HILL:

I can see that "enthusiasm" is a greatly misunderstood word, judging by what you have been telling me.

CARNEGIE:

Yes, it is perhaps the most misunderstood word in the English language. Most so-called enthusiasm is nothing but an uncontrolled expression of one's ego—a state of mental excitement which is easily recognized as nothing but a meaningless expression of personal vanity. That sort of enthusiasm may be very detrimental to those who indulge in it, as they usually express themselves in some form of exaggeration.

HILL:

Will you give more details concerning your statement that many of your employees have promoted themselves through the expression of enthusiasm? Just what effect did their enthusiasm have on their jobs that entitled them to promotion?

> *The Gothic cathedrals, the Madonnas of Raphael and Titian, the miracles of music—all sprang out of some genuine enthusiasm.*

CARNEGIE:

It not only had an effect on their own jobs, but it affected those who worked with them! A man with a negative mind, working in a plant where he may contact hundreds of other workmen, may influence all the others to become also negative to a greater or lesser degree. The same principle applies where one has a positive mind and expresses enthusiasm in connection with his work.

Any state of mind is contagious.

Now you can see why an employee with a positive mind is worth more than one with a negative mind. The employee who thinks in terms of enthusiasm naturally is one who is happy in his work. He therefore radiates a wholesome mental attitude that spreads to those around him and they, too, take on a part of his attitude. Accordingly, they become more efficient workers.

But that is not the only reason why the person who expresses enthusiasm as a habit promotes himself into the more desirable positions of life. Enthusiasm, as I have already stated, gives one a keener imagination, increases his initiative, makes him more alert of mind, gives him a more pleasing personality, and thereby attracts the cooperation of others. These traits of mind make it inevitable that one will promote himself into any position which he may become capable of filling.

Every thought one releases becomes a definite part of one's character! This transformation takes place through the principle of autosuggestion. One does not have to be a mathematician to figure out what will happen to the person whose dominating thoughts are positive, in view of the fact that such a person is adding power to his own character with every thought he releases. Thought by thought he builds a personality that provides him with a strong will, a keen imagination, self-reliance, persistence, initiative, and the courage and ambition to desire and to acquire whatever he wants. An employer has but little to do with the promotion of such a person. If one employer neglects to recognize his ability he finds another who will, but he manages to keep growing and advancing in any direction he chooses.

HILL:

I get the idea, Mr. Carnegie. An employee whose mind is dominated by the spirit of enthusiasm is beneficial to an employer, not only by his influence on other employees, but because of his own acquired strength of personality. Is that what you mean?

CARNEGIE:

That's exactly what I mean. And the principle applies to everyone; not merely to an employee. Take the owner of a retail store, for example, and you will find that his mental attitude is definitely reflected in every person who works in the store. I have heard it said that a skilled psychologist can walk through any retail store, study the employees a few minutes, and then give a surprisingly accurate description of the owner or the dominating head of the store, without ever seeing him or hearing a word spoken by him.

HILL:

Then one might say that a store, or a business, has its own "personality" consisting of the dominating influence of the personnel of the business. Is that true?

CARNEGIE:

Yes, and it is true of the home, or any place where people gather regularly. The psychologist with a keen sense of perception can walk into any home, get the "mental feel" of the place, and tell precisely whether the home is dominated by the spirit of harmony or the spirit of bickering and friction. The mental attitude of people leaves its permanent influence on the very atmosphere of their environment.

Every city, for example, has its own rate of vibration, made up of the dominating influences and the mental attitudes of the people who live there. Moreover, every street, and every block in every street, has its own "personality," each being so different from the others that the trained psychologist can walk down any street, blindfolded, and pick up enough information from the "mental feel" of the street to give an accurate description of the people who live there.

HILL:

That seems almost incredible, Mr. Carnegie.

CARNEGIE:

Perhaps it may, to the inexperienced person, but not so to the skilled interpreter of people's "mental attitude." If you wish convincing evidence of the accuracy of what I have said, make an experiment of your own. Take a walk down Fifth Avenue, in New York City, and observe the feeling of opulence you pick up as you go along. Then go across to the tenement section, take a stroll down that thoroughfare, and observe the feeling of defeatism and poverty that you will pick up. The experiment will provide you with undeniable evidence that the vibrations of Fifth Avenue and the vibrations of the tenement street are direct opposites, one negative, the other positive.

Carry the experiment still further by going into private homes. Choose a home where you know there is domestic harmony and cooperation. Study, carefully, the "mental feel" you pick up in this home, without anyone speaking a word to you. Then go into a home where you know the domestic relationship is disturbed by inharmony and family friction. Study the "mental feel" you pick up there. By the time you have made a dozen such experiments, you will know from firsthand experience that every home has a "mental atmosphere" that harmonizes perfectly with the "mental attitude" of those who live there.

This experiment will also convince you that there is some unknown law of nature which fixes the habits of thought and tends to give them permanency. The law not only gives permanency to thought, in the mind of the individual, but it extends the influence of that thought to the environment in which one lives.

HILL:

I had already noticed the difference in the "mental feel" of different homes, but I had attributed this to the financial status of the occupants. It seemed to me that poverty-stricken homes reflected a feeling of poverty on account of the physical appearance of the home, the furnishings and the like, and that the homes where there was evidence of opulence reflected a feeling of opulence because of the physical evidence of opulence. Don't you think that physical appearances have something to do with the impressions one picks up in a home?

CARNEGIE:

Physical appearances are deceiving, if one relies upon them entirely. Many people are deceived in this manner. Evidences of opulence are no indication whatsoever of mental harmony. Neither is physical evidence of poverty any definite indication of lack of mental harmony.

Do not assume, however, that physical surroundings are not important. They are important because they suggest a positive or negative mental attitude which the mind accepts and acts upon. The man who accepts an environment of poverty, as reflected by its physical surroundings, will find himself becoming poverty conscious. On the other hand, the man who demands an environment of opulence will become success conscious. The clothes one wears have a definite effect on one's mental attitude. And it has been proved that even so slight a detail as shoes with run-down heels will tend to give one a feeling of inferiority, and a soiled shirt or an unshaven face will do the same. These are facts with which everyone is familiar, although not everyone recognizes the far-reaching influence of such seemingly unimportant details.

You can drive through the country and analyze the mental habits of the farmers by observing the appearance of their land and buildings. Those who have become poverty conscious allow their farms and their buildings to become run-down and "seedy" in appearance. Evidence of this is unmistakable. The same rule applies to the city home. Take one glance at it and you can get an accurate impression of the mental attitude of those who occupy it. The evidence is reflected in the appearance of the lawn, the condition of the house, and the "feel" one gets when near the house.

HILL:

Mr. Carnegie, you have opened to me a field of thought which I fear I have never explored before. You have given me a new standard by which to analyze people, by observation of their physical surroundings and their personal appearance.

CARNEGIE:

The officials of the United States Army are very particular about the personal appearance of the soldiers under their command. They know, from experience, that slovenly men, who neglect their personal appearance and their living quarters, make poor fighters. That is why the Army and the Navy have regular inspection periods when everyone is looked over carefully. Personal appearances give an accurate insight into what takes place in the minds of men.

The same rule applies, less strictly, in the field of business. Some retail stores, for example, are so particular about the personal appearance of their salespeople that they, too, have regular inspection periods. They have learned from experience that the public judges a store very largely by the appearance of its sales-people. Many an employee has attracted attention to himself and gained promotion by his neat personal appearance. Of course, the promotion was not based on the appearance alone, but it was a determining factor that connoted other qualities which go along with personal appearance.

HILL:

Yes, I see! Personal appearances advertise one's mental attitude.

CARNEGIE:

Now you have the idea! Try as one may, he cannot separate his mental attitude from his personal appearance and his physical environment. The two are closely akin.

I wish to call your attention to the fact that this rule applies to domestic animals and to the birds and beasts of wildlife, the same as to man. The finer specimens take great care with their physical appearance. The songbirds keep their feathers clean and neatly arranged, while the more slovenly birds, such as the buzzard, pay less attention to their physical appearance. That old saying that "cleanliness is next to Godliness" is by no means a mere figure of speech. The more spirited creatures of the earth reflect the nature of their spirit by their physical appearance and their environment. This, alone, should provide man with a clue by which to govern himself.

HILL:

When you speak of "the more spirited creatures" you have reference to those which show definite signs of enthusiasm, do you not?

CARNEGIE:

Well, that would be one way of stating the matter. We might even speak of people as being either "spirited," or enthusiastic, or lacking in this quality. The habits of slovenly, unspirited people are not unlike those of the unspirited creatures of the lower planes in the animal world. Yes, I think you might say that some animals reflect the spirit of enthusiasm. Take a well-bred dog, for example, and you will see an animal that can do almost everything but talk; and a dog can talk, too, in his own way.

HILL:

Let us now consider some of the influences which discourage enthusiasm.

CARNEGIE:

Very well, let us begin by naming the more common antitheses of enthusiasm, heading the list with one of the most deadly of them all, viz.:

1. Poverty! It has been said that when poverty comes in at the front door, hope, ambition, courage, initiative, and enthusiasm take to their heels and go out at the back door.
2. Illness. It is difficult for one to display enthusiasm over anything when he is physically or mentally ill.
3. Failure in business. Those who have not learned the art of converting defeat into renewed effort usually allow failure in business to drown out their spirit of enthusiasm.
4. Disappointment in love. I have never yet seen the person who could display convincing signs of genuine enthusiasm while suffering from this sort of disappointment.

5. Family disputes. It is difficult for a man to display enthusiasm in connection with his business, profession, or occupation if he knows that an argument awaits him when he arrives at home at the end of the day.

6. Religious indecision. When a man is upset because of indecision in connection with his religious beliefs, he finds his spirit of enthusiasm dampened.

7. Fear. Enthusiasm and fear make poor bedfellows, and this has reference to all types of fear.

8. Lack of a Definite Major Purpose. The man who drifts with the stray winds of chance finds it difficult to control his enthusiasm. He usually displays enthusiasm, if at all, in connection with trivial matters that do him no permanent good. A fixed major purpose is the greatest of all the stimulants of enthusiasm. Give a man a goal around which he can build an obsessional desire for its attainment, and enthusiasm becomes a natural habit with him.

9. Lack of self-discipline. The man who allows his emotions to take possession of him is apt to become the victim of negative emotions, and these, of course, are fatal to enthusiasm.

10. Lack of Faith in Infinite Intelligence. Perhaps the most beneficial type of enthusiasm is that which is displayed by the man who has learned how to place himself in tune with the Infinite, for this type of man blends Faith with enthusiasm in such a manner that he moves with definiteness in all he does.

11. The habit of procrastination. If and when the procrastinator displays enthusiasm, it is lacking in force because there is nothing definite back of it.

12. Acting on one's individual initiative, without the cooperation of others. The Master Mind principle gives one the

most effective means of developing and applying enthusiasm. The man who lives as a "lone wolf" usually is a cynic, with little sign of enthusiasm.

13. Disloyalty of friends and business associates. This type of perfidy usually dampens one's enthusiasm, temporarily at least.

14. Lack of education. While this is greatly overestimated as a dampener of enthusiasm, it remains, however, as such in the minds of many people.

15. Lack of opportunity for self-advancement. This rates along with poverty as an enthusiasm dampener. Most people seem never to have learned how to attract opportunity through the spirit of enthusiasm.

16. Unfriendly criticism. The majority of people go into their shells of silence and place their enthusiasm on cold storage the moment they are criticized, or they become cynical and strike back at their critics.

17. Old age. Some people accept the maturity of years not as an approach to greater wisdom but as a sign of decline in ability. To the one who masters and applies this philosophy of individual achievement, maturity of years should bring increased ability, based on a better understanding and use of the mind.

18. Negative mental attitude. The habit of looking on the dark side of the circumstances of one's life is fatal to enthusiasm.

19. Doubt and worry. To be a habitual enthusiast one must be a strong believer in something! Unbelievers are negative, and unbelief becomes a habit. If one indulges it in one direction it assumes control in many directions. Worry is the child of doubt. It grows out of indecision and inaction. This is one of the commonest antitheses of enthusiasm, and

it is inexcusable because it is a habit that can be eliminated by the simple process of adopting a Definite Major Purpose and working that purpose so vigorously that there is no room in the mind for doubt.

20. The habit of associating with negative-minded people. No one can maintain a spirit of enthusiasm while fraternizing with pessimists and cynics.

21. Lack of ambition.

22. Skepticism and doubt.

23. Negative mental attitude expressed in criticism of others and of life in general.

These are the major destroyers of enthusiasm!

When the mind is dominated by any combination of these enthusiasm dampeners, it becomes negative. Enthusiasm is the product of a positive mind. I mean the sort of mind that is positive all the time, as a matter of controlled habit.

No one is doing the best of which he is capable until his work arouses all of the enthusiasm and zest of his being.

HILL:

Then it is necessary that the mind be cleared of these negative habits before enthusiasm can become a part of one's thought habits?

CARNEGIE:

Yes, enthusiasm is an expression of hope, belief, and the will to win! It cannot thrive on doubt, unbelief, and indefiniteness of purpose. Enthusiasm must be developed through action appropriate to its nature. Wishing and daydreaming will not develop enthusiasm.

When a man gets an obsessional desire to attain a definite goal, and pitches in, with everything he has, to attain it, the action feature of his desire evolves into enthusiasm.

HILL:

And enthusiasm prepares the mind for the expression of Faith?

CARNEGIE:

Developing enthusiasm involves three definite steps. First, one clears the mind thought habits. Second, one fills the mind with a Definite Major Purpose based on a motive. Third, one begins action in carrying out the purpose, and follows through so vigorously that the motive behind the purpose becomes an obsession.

Negative thought habits can be eliminated by adopting other and stronger habits of the opposite nature. Here, too, physical action plays an important part. One cannot eliminate undesirable habits by merely wishing to eliminate them. They must be supplanted by stronger habits of a desirable nature.

HILL:

There is no way, then, for one to escape work?

CARNEGIE:

A majority of the people devote much of their time avoiding work, but so far no one has been smart enough to accomplish this end without experiencing its natural consequences, failure.

HILL:

If I understand you correctly, it is your belief that work can be made a pleasure, if it is directed to a definite objective on which one has "sold" himself?

CARNEGIE:

Now you have laid your finger on the key to all successful achievement. No man can succeed, in the broader sense of the term, without finding peace of mind and happiness. If a man cannot find happiness in connection with the pursuit of his Definite Major Purpose, how would he find it? Many people make the mistake of believing that work serves only the purpose of acquiring material things, money, for example; the necessities and the luxuries of life. But the truth is that work is the only means of finding happiness. An idle person never is happy. Happiness comes from doing that which one likes best to do.

I have a great deal of money, but I tell you frankly that I get no happiness from it. Such happiness as I have experienced came from planning, building, and creating, and helping other men to find their places in the world. Money and material things do not provide fellowship except by their use in providing action for the owner. The miser never is happy, but the man who uses his material wealth to give expression to his own mind, and to aid others in expressing themselves, may become happy.

Yes, work can become a pleasure if one engages in it in the right attitude. I once asked Thomas A. Edison how he managed to work such long hours without wearing himself out. It was no surprise to me when he said, "I am so keenly interested in what I am doing that what you call work is recreation to me. My trouble is not long hours; it is the shortness of the hours. I begrudge the time I have to give over to sleep."

And he told the truth. His work has become his obsession. His interest in it is so keen that he finds happiness in it. That is the experience of every man who has found his work and is engaged in doing it, in a spirit of enthusiasm. Edison's enthusiasm takes the drudgery out of his work. That's how he manages to keep at a task through thousands of failures, until he finishes it. And that's why he is the world's greatest inventor. Inventing is his hobby. He does not "work" at it. He plays with it, and plays hard.

Observe any man who has made work an obsession and you will discover that he gets happiness from it.

HILL:

Yes, I get your viewpoint, but my mind keeps reverting to people who are born in an environment of poverty and illiteracy. I know something of that sort of environment because I was born in it. How is one going to become enthusiastic over anything when everything he sees, everyone he associates with, suggests poverty?

CARNEGIE:

I think you can answer your own question by recalling how you escaped the undesirable environment of your birth. What steps did you take? What state of mind did you develop that permitted you to choose a more desirable environment? You have plenty of enthusiasm! Very well, how did you come by it? When you have answered these questions you will have answered your own question much better than I could answer it.

HILL:

I escaped the undesirable environment of my birth because of the influence of a remarkable woman who refused to accept poverty: my stepmother. She fired my imagination with a desire to adopt a Definite Major Purpose and I followed it out of the jungle. Her enthusiasm was, as you have stated, contagious. I caught it and it became my own. But I was fortunate in having come by chance under the influence of a positive mind. Not everyone is so fortunate. What of those who are not so favored by chance? How are they to escape the deadening effects of a poverty-stricken environment?

CARNEGIE:

I am glad you have asked those questions, because I have the answer and I wish you to remember it. I have already told you that the turning point in every man's life, at which he begins to supplant the poverty consciousness and the spirit of defeatism with the will to win, is reached generally when he comes under the influence of some person with a positive mind. I will admit that in most cases this turning point is reached by a chance meeting with the right type of person; in fact, I wish to emphasize this fact. It was the recognition of this very fact which inspired me to search, over a long period of years, for a man to help me organize the philosophy of individual achievement. This philosophy, when it is completed, will serve as that necessary outside influence which a man needs to enable him to break away from anything he does not want, including a poverty consciousness.

You see, therefore, that you are being schooled to help me answer the very important question which you have asked! When the philosophy has been completely organized and tested, it will be taken to the people in the humblest environments of the nation and world. And let us not forget, as we organize the philosophy, to prepare it in terms that the humblest person can understand. In our presentation of the philosophy we must not only tell the people what they should do to escape the circumstances of life they do not wish, but we must teach them how to do it! The philosophy must be as nearly foolproof as human ingenuity can make it.

HILL:

So, my questions have kicked back on me like a boomerang!

CARNEGIE:

No, your questions have opened to me the opportunity I have been waiting for, an opportunity to impress you with the nature of the responsibility you have undertaken. I want you to follow through with your job with the feeling that you are to become a liberator of poverty-bound people. You are preparing yourself to help people unlock the prison doors of their own minds, where they have confined themselves by their self-imposed limitations. Look upon your job in this light and you'll never have any need to worry about your own enthusiasm, unless it is to save you from driving yourself too hard and fast.

Now may I tell you something that should give you great satisfaction? You were chosen as my emissary, to help prepare the philosophy of individual achievement for the people of America and the world, not alone because of your alertness in recognizing and acting upon the opportunity when I offered it to you, but for the further reason that the background of your humble birth has prepared you to recognize the need for an inspirational philosophy designed to awaken people and help them throw off their poverty consciousness.

You know what poverty is because you have lived in it!

You know what opulence is because you are now beginning to enjoy it. Most important of all, you know the way out of poverty; or you will know the way out by the time you finish your job in organizing the philosophy of individual achievement.

Thus you have found in your own experience one of the greatest evidences of the soundness of the theory that "adversity brings with it the seed of an equivalent benefit." Your greatest opportunity grew out of the handicap under which you were born. I wish you to be impressed by this. I wish you to impress others with this same thought, for it is one of the most important facts of life. Its importance becomes obvious to its fullest degree in the time of emergency, when one is overtaken by defeat and one's enthusiasm has been wiped out. The person who has mastered this philosophy will not only discover that defeat is only temporary, but he will know, at the time of defeat, that somewhere in connection with it there is the seed of an equivalent victory, and he will begin to search for that seed. Thus discouragement can be converted into enthusiasm!

HILL:

So, I can see by the twinkle in your eyes that you deliberately led me into asking a question that gave you an opening to teach me a lesson?

CARNEGIE:

I must confess that you are right. Yes, I have been waiting for just this moment to catch you off guard, so I could help you convert doubt into Faith. I have known for some time that you were worrying about how people who are born in a negative environment may escape. Your worry was the child of your own experience, and you are not yet far enough removed from the environment in which you were born to enable you to throw off its effects. Let that give you no further concern. From now on you will be associated with men who are success conscious, and their influence will give you hope and Faith, for you will discover that every one of them went through some sort of experience similar to your own before they took possession of their own minds.

Yes, I did set a trap for you, and I am glad you fell into it, for it gave me an opportunity to force you to become your own teacher, on a subject of the greatest importance in connection with the job that lies ahead of you. In the future when you tell anyone that "adversity brings with it the seed of an equivalent benefit" you may speak from your own experience. What you say will be more convincing to others because it will be based on what you know; not what you have heard. I have still other traps prepared for you, so be on the lookout!

HILL:

Am I to understand, from what you have said, that people who are born in a poverty-stricken environment can escape only through the influence of someone with a positive mind?

CARNEGIE:

Oh no! Some people are born with an inherent nature which drives them to find their own means of escape from poverty, and they begin searching for the way out as soon as they are thrown on their own responsibility.

HILL:

But they find the way out much sooner if they have the aid of people who inspire them with ambition and confidence. Is that the idea?

CARNEGIE:

Yes, that is true, but it has been my experience that even those who begin to search for a way to master poverty, and find it, usually contact someone, sooner or later, who inspires them with imagination, initiative, or some other quality that is instrumental in helping them. I do not recall having ever known of anyone succeeding, in a noteworthy degree, without the influence of one or more people who aided him. Whatever success I have attained has been due, largely, to the aid I received from others.

HILL:

Do you advocate the habit of one's relying on others for aid, or should one move on his own initiative?

CARNEGIE:

The man who moves on his own initiative has a much better chance of succeeding than the one who depends on others.

When a man wishes to do something, he should begin on his own initiative, and work with whatever tools he may have at hand. He will come into possession of greater resources in proportion to his use of his own available resources. The world does not favor the person who depends too greatly upon others for his own promotion. I once saw a motto which impressed me very much. It said, "Some people succeed when encouraged by others, while a few succeed in spite of the devil and all his angels." I rather like the latter part of the motto. Encouragement from others is a great benefit; encouragement from one's self is an indispensable necessity.

HILL:

What encouragement have you for the man who is born with a will to win, but lacks the inherent quality of enthusiasm?

You know, of course, there are such people. Are they doomed to failure?

CARNEGIE:

Now you have come dangerously near to setting your foot into another trap by your question. I have answered this question for you previously. I want you to answer that question for yourself.

HILL:

Yes, of course! You mean that the Master Mind principle provides one with the medium by which any individual deficiency may be bridged. Isn't that what you have in mind, Mr. Carnegie?

CARNEGIE:

Precisely! I can name for you a dozen men who show no signs of active enthusiasm, yet they are succeeding in their chosen calling. They have been wise enough to include in their Master Mind group one or more who have the necessary capacity for enthusiasm. I have several men in my Master Mind group who are entirely lacking in the quality of enthusiasm; so much so, in fact, that one of them is known as the "wet blanket" man of the group. We have him in the group for that purpose. It is his business to find out the plans which will not work. He questions everything and everyone. If he ever smiles it is while he is asleep. But he is one of our most valuable men. He would be less valuable, however, if we did not have others in the group who, by their enthusiasm, put their imaginations to work and create plans and ideas. It is very seldom that the creator of an idea can be the best critic of its merits.

HILL:

It seems to me that I may have led you into a trap, Mr. Carnegie, for you have just admitted that a man may become an important part of an organization without enthusiasm!

CARNEGIE:

Think again, for you have overlooked the fact that I said we have men in our Master Mind group who supply enthusiasm. Well, the man without enthusiasm profits by his association with those who have it, just as they profit by their association with him. He needs their ideas; they need his "balancing" influence.

HILL:

I see what you mean. The man without enthusiasm probably would not be so valuable if he moved solely on his own initiative.

CARNEGIE:

That's the idea that springs your trap for me. And now may I call your attention to the fact that you've just walked into the trap you thought you were setting for me? You now have a viewpoint in connection with the Master Mind principle which I have been trying to impress upon you. You know that a Master Mind group should consist of creators of ideas and critics of ideas, both types working in harmony. Every Master Mind group should have at least one "wet blanket" man to test the ideas of the others. Only in this way can you have "balanced" enthusiasm.

One of the weaknesses of most individuals who are inspired by enthusiasm is their lack of a dependable means of controlling their enthusiasm, through the influence of a constructive critic.

> *An enthusiastic workman*
> *dignifies his art and arrives at results.*

HILL:

I get your idea, Mr. Carnegie, and I shall not forget to include it in the philosophy of individual achievement. I fear it is the lack of understanding of the point you have explained which accounts for the poor judgment so many men use in choosing their business associates.

CARNEGIE:

Now you are doing some real analyzing. I have seen it proved, over and over again, that failure in business is generally due to the wrong association of men. Modern industry is so complex it requires many types of men to manage it successfully. The business that is loaded too heavily with one type of man has two strikes against it to begin with.

HILL:

How do you manage to keep your "wet blanket" man from killing off the enthusiasm of your idea men?

CARNEGIE:

In a well-managed business it is understood that both types of men have a place; that both are necessary for the successful operation of the business. You understand, of course, that professional criticism is a far different thing from voluntary, uninvited criticism, such as some men offer to others in social relationships. Professional criticism is, or should be, accepted as friendly analysis intended to benefit all whom it influences. Personal criticism usually is nothing but an expression of disapproval, often based on antagonism.

HILL:

You believe, then, that an employer should be subject to friendly criticism from his employees?

CARNEGIE:

If he is not, he is not getting the best service from those who work with him. Employers who surround themselves with "yes-men"—as many do—seldom succeed, and they never attain the success they might enjoy if they invited friendly criticism.

HILL:

Your analysis is very revealing, Mr. Carnegie. I am beginning to see what you meant when you said that your greatest contribution to the steel industry, of which you are the recognized head, consists in your ability to pick men who can and will do what is required of them. If I have judged your remarks correctly, you are now coaching me in the art of building an organization of efficient men. Is that your idea?

CARNEGIE:

That is exactly what I am doing. The philosophy of individual achievement will fail in its mission unless it clearly explains the proper approach to all human relationships. Human relationship is the most important subject in the world. Success and failure both hinge upon it. The greatest service that any educational system can render anyone is that of teaching him how to negotiate his way through life with a minimum of opposition from others. This is far more important than training in the arts and sciences. Men who are skilled in the arts and sciences are plentiful. They can be employed for wages. Men who are skilled at forming harmonious human relationships are scarce. Remember that the major burden of the philosophy of individual achievement is that of training men to relate themselves to others in a spirit of harmony, and in the ability to influence others to do the same.

HILL:

I understand what you mean, Mr. Carnegie. I also understand much more about the subject of enthusiasm than I did when we began this discussion. The subject cannot be satisfactorily treated as a single unit; it is related to other principles of this philosophy which must be applied with it in order to make it effective as a means of promoting one's individual interests.

CARNEGIE:

Now you are gaining an understanding of the philosophy with a true perspective. Every principle of the philosophy is related to every other principle. The principles are interlocking, like the links of a chain. Enthusiasm, for example, is directly related to the principles of self-discipline, attractive personality, organized endeavor, and organized thought. Remove self-discipline from enthusiasm, and you are dealing with a force that may serve only to lead one into dangerous habits of exaggeration.

HILL:

That word "habit" creeps into this philosophy quite often, too!

CARNEGIE:

Yes, and so does the word "action." Both are key words. Habits are developed through the repetition of action, and this applies to mental habits as well as to physical habits. Advertising men have learned that the repetition of ideas is an essential for successful advertisements. Millions of dollars are spent annually for the sole purpose of emphasizing the names of products, by repetition. If the principle of repetition is sound in advertising, it is sound in other connections.

Some men never hear what is said the first time an idea is mentioned. If it is repeated, they may think they heard some sort of noise; but they will not be certain what it meant. If it is repeated again, they will catch a vague notion of what was said. If it is repeated a fourth time, they may hear clearly what was said, but not be impressed by it. Perhaps by the time the idea is repeated a fifth time it may sink into their consciousness, but it will not remain there unless it is repeated many times thereafter.

I am speaking, of course, of new ideas. People take to new ideas slowly and they usually show antagonism to new ideas when they first hear of them. Only the trained, self-disciplined, alert mind is capable of accepting a new idea when it is first introduced. This type of mind is scarce. Remember what I have said when you wish to get a new idea across.

HILL:

I can think of three words, Mr. Carnegie, which are heard and understood the first time they are spoken. They are the three little words that men sometimes speak to women: "I love you."

CARNEGIE:

Yes, but the idea back of them is not new! It is as old as the human race. Even these words need to be repeated often or they lose their meaning. If you doubt it, observe the man who has stopped telling his wife or his sweetheart that he loves her. Perhaps the spirit of romance provides more enthusiasm than any other subject in the world, but it withers and dies unless it is kept alive by the repetition of words and deeds. The same may be said of the spirit of friendship. The man who neglects to proclaim his feeling of friendship, by words and deeds, soon finds himself without friends. You see, not even the great spirit of friendship can live without action to support it.

HILL:

That is only another way of saying that everything has its price, and nothing can be gained that is of permanent value unless the price is paid.

CARNEGIE:

Nothing! Not even love or friendship. The man who believes that either of these important human relationships is free deceives himself. In fact, there is no other relationship which requires as careful nursing as these. The moment one stops feeding them with words and deeds, they die.

HILL:

I had no intention of diverting your analysis of enthusiasm to discussion of love.

CARNEGIE:

Man alive! You haven't. You have brought up a subject which inspires more enthusiasm than anything I could mention. Take enthusiasm out of love and friendship, and you have nothing left. These are among the highest forms of inspired feeling.

HILL:

One might carry the illustration a step further by saying, "Take love and friendship out of the world, and you would have nothing left worth fighting for."

CARNEGIE:

Yes, those relationships are associated with the highest achievements of civilization. If a man had no friends and loved no one, he might as well go back to the primitive state and join the beasts of the jungle.

HILL:

I never thought of enthusiasm as being an essential part of one's aesthetic nature, but I can see that it is.

CARNEGIE:

Not merely a part of it, but practically the whole of it. Man's capacity to enjoy or to create artistic things is, of itself, a form of enthusiasm. You will see that it is if you remember that enthusiasm is nothing but a highly concentrated form of feeling. Therefore it is directly related to all the positive emotions.

HILL:

Then enthusiasm is the action feature of the mind which inspires all constructive effort and gives action to all positive motives.

CARNEGIE:

Now you are beginning to comprehend what I have been trying to convey to you. Now you recognize why Emerson said, "Nothing great was ever achieved without enthusiasm." His statement was founded on a deep understanding of the power of enthusiasm, for he must have known that it is the action feature of all positive thoughts and all constructive effort.

HILL:

Yes, I understand, now, why you emphasized the necessity of one's adopting an obsessional motive as the foundation of one's Definite Major Purpose in life. An obsessional motive is one behind which has been placed the feeling of enthusiasm. Is that it?

CARNEGIE:

You understand it correctly. Take care that you understand, also, that enthusiasm can be developed, like any other habit, by the control of one's mental and physical habits.

HILL:

Your analysis has given me the answer to a question that has puzzled me for a long while. I have observed that the average public speaker has to go through what he calls the "warming-up" period, during the first few minutes of his speech, before he shows signs of enthusiasm. From what you have said about the relationship between enthusiasm and action, I draw the conclusion that the "warming-up" process consists of the coordination of thought with the physical expression of words; that thought is intensified until it becomes enthusiasm, through physical expression.

CARNEGIE:

Well, that's a new idea to me, but I have the feeling you are right. There is another factor in connection with public speaking which had never occurred to me before. I have observed that the greatest brilliancy of thought is attained by the public speaker when his enthusiasm is at its highest pitch. Therefore it is obvious that enthusiasm stimulates the imagination, makes one's memory more alert, and perhaps gives the public speaker direct connection with Infinite Intelligence, through the subconscious section of the mind, under certain conditions when his enthusiasm is at a high pitch. I had long ago observed that the subconscious mind acts more quickly on ideas that are created under highly emotional conditions.

HILL:

Your analysis suggests the idea that the state of mind known as Faith is directly related to the emotional feeling of enthusiasm.

CARNEGIE:

Yes, it does. Intense enthusiasm probably steps up the rate of thought vibration so that the conscious mind may connect directly with Infinite Intelligence. If this theory is correct, it would account for the fact that prayer sometimes brings the desired results while at other times it brings no results at all. It seems to be the consensus of opinion of all to whom I have talked about prayer that it never produces desired results unless it is accompanied by Faith. We have reason to believe that the emotional feeling of enthusiasm clears the mind of thought impulses which prevent Faith.

Now let me call your attention to the fact that this theory (if it is no more than a theory) applies also to circumstances other than prayer. For example, when one adopts the habit of Definiteness of Purpose and applies it in connection with all of his daily routine, he very soon reaches the point at which he expects the object of his desires to be attained. By concentrating his thoughts upon his desires, he is usually rewarded, in due time, by Faith in his ability to get what he desires. Now, the important feature I wish you to observe is the fact that ordinary desire becomes absolute Faith in proportion that one intensifies his desire by his enthusiasm! When enthusiasm becomes so great that it enables one to have enough Faith to see (in his imagination) the object of his desires already in his possession, even before he actually has obtained physical possession, he experiences precisely the same results that he would obtain if he called his desires prayer. The name one gives to this mysterious power is unimportant! It brings results under one name as well as under any other. The state of mind in which one approaches the subject is the really important thing. Fear, doubt, indefiniteness, and lack of enthusiasm produce negative results, always, in connection with the principle of desire. If the mind is dominated by any one of these negatives, the results of desire will be negative. On this point I can be definite for I have made a lifetime study of the subject in connection with my own experiences and the experiences of many others.

*

Since the persistent man is likely to have what he desires, be sure to ask only for the things that are best.

It is impressively significant that the lack of enthusiasm ends in negative results in connection with both the principle of Definiteness of Purpose and the more formal expression of desires known as prayer.

HILL:

Then the person who is incapable of developing enthusiasm is hopelessly handicapped, is he not?

CARNEGIE:

No, I wouldn't state it that strongly. The word "hopeless" is very final. It is almost as final as the word "death." I do not like to think of any circumstance as hopeless beyond cure.

The person who cannot or will not develop enthusiasm may still find hope in the Master Mind principle, through which he may obtain the benefits of minds that can develop enthusiasm.

He may also avail himself of the aid of doctors of suggestive therapeutics, in extreme cases of melancholy and hypochondria (imaginary illness), and gain relief from the condition which prevents the free flow of thought that is necessary in developing enthusiasm. It has been discovered that "ill temper," negative mental attitude, indifference, laziness, and the lack of alertness of the mind in general often are the result of some physical condition which can be corrected. These conditions are also traceable, oftentimes, to some quirk in the mental equipment of the brain which can be corrected by suggestive therapeutics (a mild application of hypnotism), and by autosuggestion applied by the individual, provided he understands the operations of the mind and has a will to correct evils that prevent its normal operations.

HILL:

It appears that enthusiasm and sound health have much in common.

CARNEGIE:

Yes, you might go further and say that whenever one is lacking in enthusiasm it should be a sign for him to look after his physical health, for there is where he will find the cause. People of normal health (physical and mental health) seldom are lacking in enthusiasm. An alert mind cannot function in a dull, sluggish body.

HILL:

What about the habit of drinking alcoholic beverages? Is that not one of the destroyers of enthusiasm?

CARNEGIE:

The habit does more than destroy enthusiasm. First it inspires greater enthusiasm, but the reaction, known as "the morning after," is the real destroyer. The physical body manufactures its own alcohol, in such quantities as it needs. Beyond this amount any alcohol that is taken into the body may become a poison that breaks down bodily resistance. The only safe stimulant of the physical body (outside of the stimulants applied by physicians in medical treatment) is mental stimulation, through inspiration and enthusiasm. That sort of stimulation has no detrimental physical reactions. It is nature's medicine. If it becomes a habit, it is a beneficial habit, which is more than can be said of any artificial stimulant, such as drugs or alcohol.

HILL:

Then you condemn the use of narcotics and alcohol?

CARNEGIE:

Absolutely! Unless they are administered under the direction of a reputable physician who uses them for medicinal purposes, in treating people who are ill.

HILL:

You wouldn't recommend even a social drink?

CARNEGIE:

Social drinks might do no harm if they were taken in moderation, but too many people begin the alcohol habit by an occasional social drink. It is safe to remain a teetotaler!

HILL:

I have heard that some very great authors, musicians, and poets did their best work under the influence of alcohol. Such men as Edgar Allan Poe, Robert Burns, James Whitcomb Riley, and Stephen Foster.

CARNEGIE:

Yes, perhaps they did good work under the influence of liquor, but do not overlook the tragedy of their lives. We know of a part of that tragedy, but not all of it. Liquor and sound minds do not harmonize. Intoxicating liquor will stimulate the action of the brain, but the reaction will be the equivalent of the action. It will consist of headaches and dulled faculties of the mind. If this sort of mind stimulation becomes a habit, it will destroy the capacity for inspired feeling, which is nature's method of stimulating the mind with a natural energy that leaves no unfavorable effects. One may become highly intoxicated with enthusiasm, but that sort of intoxication leaves no headaches behind it, nor does it destroy the capacity of the brain to respond to the stimuli that inspire enthusiasm.

HILL:

It seems, then, that when man substitutes his method of stimulating the brain, for that already provided by nature, he pays a penalty for his mistake by having nature's method withheld from him. Is that what you mean?

CARNEGIE:

That's it! Nature penalizes interference with her methods of functioning, not only in the matter of mind stimulation, but in all other respects. For example, nature provides a covering of hair for protection of the head, but if a man tries to improve her handiwork by supplementing it with a covering of his own, consisting of a tight-fitting hat that cuts off the circulation of the blood from the roots of the hair, nature penalizes the interference with baldness.

Nature does precisely the same thing when man substitutes his own methods of brain stimulation, by the use of alcohol and narcotics, but in this case she looks with particular disfavor on man's efforts, because she not only penalizes him with headaches and toxic poisoning, but she fastens habits upon him which blind him by his own folly! If you have ever known intimately a person who was suffering from the habit of alcoholism or narcotics you recognize what a terrible punishment nature visits upon the individual who substitutes artificial stimulants for nature's method of stimulating the brain. Finally, if the habit is continued, nature takes the supreme toll for violation of her laws, by causing illness or even death. Thus it seems obvious that the brain is one part of the physical body that cannot be interfered with without penalties which no one can afford to pay.

HILL:

Yes, I understand what you mean. Moreover, your analysis has given me an entirely new and better understanding of the nature of the damage one does himself when he stimulates his brain through negative thoughts. I can see that nature penalizes one for his lack of Faith by fastening on him his habits of unbelief!

CARNEGIE:

And the same principle applies to one's mental attitude, no matter what its nature may be. If it is positive, nature rewards one with the benefits of a positive mind, by the law of habit, through which the benefits may become permanent. If the mental attitude is negative, nature penalizes one for his mistake, through that same law of habit.

HILL:

Then nature appears not to overlook anything a man thinks or does?

CARNEGIE:

No, not even a single thought. Every thought one releases and every physical act in which he engages becomes a part of his own character.

HILL:

Obviously, then, the man whose dominating thoughts are negative reaches the point, eventually, at which most of his physical action is negative?

CARNEGIE:

That is the way nature works! And that accounts for the fact that there are so many people who have no capacity for enthusiasm. They have destroyed their capacity for mind stimulation through natural media of stimuli. Many such people turn to liquor and narcotics, vainly believing these artificial stimulants will benefit them. The truth is that such stimulants serve only the purpose of fastening the penalty upon them more firmly. The man who tries to escape fear, worry, or sorrow, by the use of artificial stimulants, meets with precisely the same experience as the man who tries to get out of quicksand by trying to pull himself out. Each effort sinks him a little deeper.

HILL:

I never imagined that liquor had anything to do with indifference and the lack of enthusiasm, but I can see, from your analysis, that it has.

CARNEGIE:

If you will study any person who is just recovering from the effects of liquor, you will know that he has been damaged, not benefited. The distorted expression on his face; his red, blurred eyes; his "ill temper"; his dull imagination; his nervousness; his upset stomach and loss of appetite—all tell a story that cannot be ignored.

On the other hand, observe any person whose brain has been stimulated by obsessional desire, or enthusiasm, or any other form of inspiration, and take note of the condition of his mind. Here you will find calmness, poise, sparkling eyes, musical tone of voice, softened lines in the face, and general alertness of the mind.

Such observations can have no other effect than that of convincing one that nature penalizes all methods of mind stimulation except those associated with inspired feeling. There simply is no escape from this conclusion.

HILL:

Yes, I have made such observations, Mr. Carnegie, and I have noticed that your illustration applies to the man who stimulates his mind with anger, fear, revenge, jealousy, or any other negative emotion, the same as to the person who uses alcohol.

CARNEGIE:

That is precisely correct, and I wish to call your attention to the fact that all these habits, whether positive or negative, leave their marks of identification indelibly fixed on the features of the face and in the tone of the voice. That is another way nature has of rewarding or penalizing one for the use he makes of his prerogative power of thought. She clearly paints a picture of one's mental habits on one's face, so the whole world may be warned of a man's nature. Glassy eyes, harsh, irritable tones of the voice, hard lines in the face, snarly curve of the lips, nervous movements of the body all combine to inform the world that an individual is not at peace within his own mind.

HILL:

Your analysis gives me the thought that it might pay one handsomely to look himself over very carefully, in a mirror, to make sure that he is not deceiving himself as to his own mental attitude.

CARNEGIE:

That would be an excellent plan if a man would learn to read the signs I have mentioned. But there is another signal by which a man may get an accurate clue as to the real nature of his mental attitude. It is his own inner feeling. Enthusiasm, hope, and self-reliance are the natural assets of a self-disciplined person. Where these states of mind are lacking, there is something that needs investigation! There is never an exception to this rule. The man who is at peace with himself and with the world never goes to bed without some degree of hope associated with the unborn to-morrow. On this point every person should test himself every day. Where hope is missing, something has taken its place that needs to be removed. It is obvious that nature has provided every person with an accurate means of self-analysis, in this simple test which discloses hope or the lack of it.

HILL:

I had never thought of hope in that manner, Mr. Carnegie. Now that you have mentioned it, I can recall from my own limited experience that you are right. Your revelation gives me a better understanding also of the principle of Definiteness of Purpose. If one has a Definite Major Purpose, it serves to provide him with the means of testing himself on a great many qualities, such as self-reliance, initiative, imagination, self-discipline, creative vision, organized thought, and many other essential qualities. Anytime a man finds himself without hope for the attainment of his Definite Major Purpose it should serve as a warning to him that some necessary trait of mind is missing; some damaging habit has begun to take hold on him. Is that the idea?

CARNEGIE:

You've stated it perfectly. Hope is the forerunner of Faith. Where there is no hope, there can be no Faith. You can be sure that where there is no enthusiasm there is no hope, for the two are closely related. As a matter of fact, enthusiasm is a definite expression of hope! First comes hope, which is the result of desire; then follows an expression of hope, through enthusiasm; those ripen into Faith, the state of mind that masters all forms of defeat and overcomes all obstacles standing between one and the attainment of his Definite Major Purpose or his minor purposes which lead to the attainment of his major purpose.

You see, therefore, that hope, enthusiasm, and Faith are key words with a stupendous meaning because of their close relationship with one another and the circumstances of life which we call success. Where one of these is missing, success is not possible.

HILL:

That is the equivalent of saying that success requires enthusiasm?

CARNEGIE:

Exactly! Success narrows itself down to the question of one's state of mind, and we have seen clearly, I hope, that no state of mind is more important than enthusiasm. Obsessional desire and enthusiasm are synonymous terms. When one speaks of a burning desire, he means a desire that is backed by enthusiasm. We know that this is the sort of desire that inspires creative vision, personal initiative, self-reliance, Definiteness of Purpose, and all the other qualities that are indispensable for successful achievement.

HILL:

I never knew, before, that enthusiasm had so many relatives. Why, it seems to be related to all the positive qualities of the mind.

CARNEGIE:

Yes, and you might have observed, also, that it is a powerful deterrent to all the negative qualities of the mind. It serves, therefore, not only as a mind stimulant, but also helps to police the mind against the intrusion of negative habits.

HILL:

This explains, then, why "a hearty laugh a day keeps the old-man blues away"?

I also recall that most people who smile when they speak usually speak only of things that are constructive.

CARNEGIE:

You might carry your observations a little further and discover that people who smile habitually, even when they are not speaking, thereby announce to the world that their dominating thoughts are positive. By carrying your observation still further you will learn that coordination between mental attitude and physical action, when one smiles, produces a desirable change in the working of the brain.

The theory I am here analyzing explains, also, why forced physical exercise, such as one gets in the gymnasium, does less good than exercise one gets when playing a game in which he takes a keen interest, where there is coordination between mind and body.

HILL:

Your explanation reminds me that motive is an important factor in everything one does. I recall, now, that the exercise my father forced me to take as a means of punishment for misconduct involved no more labor than was required when I went on a fishing trip, but the effects were vastly different.

CARNEGIE:

Of course! The forced labor had no enthusiasm back of it. The fishing trip did have. There was coordination of body and mind on the fishing trip, but none in connection with the forced labor. And I suspect that you could have done ten times as much actual physical labor on the fishing trip as you did in the performance of the forced labor, with less feeling of fatigue.

Any physical action one takes, in a spirit of enthusiasm, requires less energy than the same action would require if the enthusiasm were not present.

HILL:

You mean, of course, that one's mental attitude modifies the physical energy one uses in all forms of physical movement?

CARNEGIE:

Yes, and you need not go any further than to analyze the difference in the energy one uses in work and in play, to recognize that mental attitude is a very important factor in the loss or the preservation of physical energy. Enthusiasm takes the drudgery out of labor, no matter what one may be doing. For this reason everyone should devote some time daily to recreation through some sort of action in which he takes a keen interest. That old saying that "all work and no play makes Jack a dull boy" is no mere figure of speech. It is based on sound psychology.

HILL:

But what of the man who likes his work better than any sort of play? Does it not serve as recreation for him?

CARNEGIE:

Yes, to a certain extent it does, but everyone should have a change of both his mental habits and his physical action, if he desires to maintain sound health. A man should learn to play as vigorously as he works. Moreover, he should learn to switch his entire mind from work to play. This is a form of self-discipline that is required for sound health. I have known men who took their work to bed with them at night, but most of them did not live the average span of years. Here is one of the circumstances which call for sufficient self-discipline to enable one to switch his motives from work to play without the loss of enthusiasm.

The physical body requires variety in both thought and physical action, the same as it requires variety of food. The man who lives on one plane, and works under one set of conditions always, comes finally to be what we call "eccentric." He loses his sense of proportion, and with it much of his self-discipline. A man should be so flexible that he can change from one mental attitude to another, and switch from one sort of physical action to another, at will, without losing his poise. In this manner only can one break the daily rhythm of his routine, and escape fixed habits by which he would otherwise be bound.

For many years I have made it a part of my daily routine to switch my mind from my major purpose to some totally disassociated purpose. Sometimes I play golf. At other times I listen to music, preferably a symphony. At other times I read. But always I find time at least once every working day to put aside all thoughts that are related to my major purpose in life. I find that by doing this my mind is fresh and alert when it comes back to the major purpose. Therefore it is more efficient.

About the saddest creature on earth is the child who, because of economic pressure or otherwise, is reared without the privilege of playing. The damaging effects of that sort of life will go with a child all through life. The human being is so created that he requires continuous change of habits in order to maintain sound health and remain happy. It is the natural response to this part of man's nature which causes everyone to like to travel. Travel brings change of thoughts, gives one "mental rest."

HILL:

This analysis has carried me into pretty deep water, Mr. Carnegie, but I must confess that it has given me a much better understanding of the part enthusiasm plays in one's life. Above all, it has shown me that sustained enthusiasm calls for variation of thought and physical action. Also, that the monotony of routine can destroy the capacity for enthusiasm. So, when I play in the future I will play with a beneficial purpose in mind.

CARNEGIE:

That's precisely the point I wished you to understand. Everything one does should be done with Definiteness of Purpose, because this adds enthusiasm to one's efforts. Only in this way can enthusiasm become a habit, as it obviously does when one mixes it with both his work and his play.

HILL:

You believe, then, that enthusiasm without plan or purpose back of it is useless?

CARNEGIE:

Not only useless, but it may be very dangerous! Enthusiasm should be under the strict control of self-discipline, the same as any other emotion.

HILL:

You believe that the self-discipline should consist in voluntary habits appropriate for the development and control of enthusiasm?

CARNEGIE:

Yes, habit is the only method of self-discipline one can control.

ANALYSIS OF CHAPTER TWO

By Napoleon Hill

Enthusiasm is one of man's greatest assets.

It beats money and power and influence. Single-handed the enthusiast convinces and dominates where the wealth accumulated by a small army of workers would scarcely raise a tremor of interest.

Enthusiasm tramples over prejudice and opposition, spurns inaction, storms the citadel of its object, and like an avalanche overwhelms and engulfs all obstacles.

It is nothing more nor less than faith in action.

Faith and initiative rightly combined remove mountainous barriers and achieve the unheard of and miraculous.

Set the germ of enthusiasm afloat in your plant, in your office, or on your farm: carry it in your attitude and manner, it spreads and influences every fiber of your industry before you realize it; it means increase in production and decrease in costs: it means joy and pleasure, and satisfaction to your workers; it means life, real, virile; it means spontaneous bedrock results—the vital things that pay dividends—throughout life.

—HENRY CHESTER

. . .

One cannot read Mr. Carnegie's analysis of the importance of enthusiasm without recognizing that it is a vital energy that is related to all creative effort.

The analysis convinces one, too, that enthusiasm is something vastly greater than mere optimism or hopeful wishing or daydreaming.

> *The mind travels faster than lightning, electricity, or radio. Light travels 186,000 miles a second. The mind can travel to the most distant star in no time that can be measured.*

Make a cross-section analysis of any number of people you choose, study the circumstances of their daily lives carefully, and you will find that those who have developed a high degree of enthusiasm enjoy more of the "breaks" of life than do those who have little or no enthusiasm.

But what is the secret behind this strange fact? Why does enthusiasm attract favorable opportunities, remove opposition, and create harmonious human relationships wherever it touches? I shall endeavor to give the answer.

Every philosopher and every thinker has discovered that enthusiasm gives added meaning to words and changes the meaning of deeds, and some have discovered that it gives greater power to thought as well as to the spoken word.

"I have heard an experienced counsellor say," remarked Emerson, "that he feared never the effect upon a jury of a lawyer who does not believe in his heart that his client ought to have a verdict. If he does not believe it, his unbelief will appear to the jury, despite all his protestations, and will become their unbelief."

Lilian Whiting caught the spirit and meaning of enthusiasm when she said, "No one has success until he has the abounding life. This is made up of the many-fold activity of energy, enthusiasm and gladness. It is to spring to meet the day with a thrill at being alive. It is to go forth to meet the morning in an ecstasy of joy. It is to realize the oneness of humanity in true spiritual sympathy."

And it was enthusiasm that William Lloyd Garrison had in mind when he said, "I am aware that many object to the severity (enthusiasm) of my language; but is there not cause for severity? I will be as harsh as Truth, and as uncompromising as Justice. On this subject I do not wish to think, or speak, or write, with moderation (without enthusiasm). No! No! Tell a man whose house is on fire to give a moderate alarm (an alarm without enthusiasm); tell him to moderately rescue his wife from the hands of the ravisher; tell the mother to gradually extricate her babe from the fire into which it has fallen— but urge me not to use moderation in a cause like the present. I am earnest (enthusiastic). I will not equivocate—I will not excuse—I will be heard. The apathy of the people is enough to make every statue leap from its pedestal and hasten the resurrection of the dead."

Observe how those words of the great Garrison move one with

feeling, although they were spoken many decades ago. The secret of their power is the enthusiasm with which they were spoken, for, as Mr. Carnegie has so impressively stated, the exact feeling in which words are expressed goes with them into the printed page, no matter if they are translated into other languages, no matter how many times they are reprinted.

Philip James Bailey understood the power of enthusiasm when he said:

> *We live in deeds, not years; in thoughts, not breaths;*
> *In feelings, not in figures on a dial.*
> *We should count time by heartthrobs.*
> *He most lives*
> *Who thinks most, feels the noblest, acts the best.*

Yes, that is true, and one "feels the noblest, acts the best" under the inspiration of enthusiasm, which helps us take inventory of the circumstances of life wherever we may and then take action.

Leigh Hunt understood the meaning of enthusiasm when he said, "There are two worlds: the world that we can measure with line and rule, and the world that we feel with our hearts and imagination."

Fichte disclosed his deep understanding of the power of enthusiasm in these words:

> *My philosophy makes life—the system of feelings and desires—*
> *supreme; and leaves knowledge merely the post of observer. This*
> *system of feelings is a fact in our minds about which there can be no*
> *dispute, a fact of which we have intuitive knowledge, a knowledge not*
> *inferred by arguments, nor generated by reasonings which can be re-*
> *ceived or neglected as we choose. Only such face-to-face knowledge*
> *has reality. It alone can get life into motion, since it springs from life.*

Terence recognized the power of enthusiasm when he said, "You believe that easily which you hope for earnestly."

James A. Garfield expressed his understanding of enthusiasm in these words: "If wrinkles must be written upon our brows let them not be written upon the heart. The spirit should not grow old." He understood that the heart is the seat of enthusiasm, the source of emotional feeling.

Tacitus said, "Adversity has no friends," and he spoke the truth, but he might well have said that adversity discourages friendships because it usually sours the emotions and dampens enthusiasm.

Froebel revealed his deep understanding of the power of enthusiasm when he said, "The delusive idea that men merely toil and work for the sake of their bodies and procuring for themselves bread, houses, and clothes, is degrading and not to be encouraged. The true origin of man's activities is his unceasing impulse to embody outside himself the divine and ritual element within him."

Those who are informed in metaphysics know that material circumstances mean nothing; that material circumstances shape themselves to fit the state of one's mind as naturally as water flows downhill in response to the law of gravitation.

The metaphysicist knows that the death of a dear friend or loved one need not bring sorrow, but it may serve as an inspiration to nobler efforts and deeper thinking, through the principle of transmutation of emotional feeling.

Emerson revealed his understanding of metaphysics in the following expressions of his thought:

A fever, a mutilation, a cruel disappointment, a loss of wealth, a loss of friends seems at the moment unpaid loss, and unpayable. But the sure years reveal the deep remedial force that underlies all facts. The death of a dear friend, wife, brother, lover, which seemed nothing but privation, somewhat later assumes the aspect of a guide or genius; for it commonly operates revolutions in our way of life, terminates an epoch of infancy or youth which was waiting to be closed, breaks up a wonted occupation, or a household, or style of living, and allows the formation of new ones more friendly to the growth of character. It permits or constrains the formation of new acquaintances, and the reception of new influences that prove of the first importance to the next years, and the man or woman who would have remained a sunny garden flower, with no room for its roots and too much sunshine for its head, by the falling of the walls and the neglect of the gardener, is made the banyan of the forest, yielding shade and fruit to wide neighborhoods of men.

One cannot get the full benefit of this chapter without recognizing the close relationship between positive and negative emotions, and the astounding possibilities of conversion of the negative into the positive. Once this possibility is understood, it will become clear that the confirmed pessimist may, by a change of his mental attitude, become a profound optimist, with the ability to express enthusiasm in exact proportion that he expressed pessimism.

Mr. Carnegie has made frequent references to the desirability of one's taking possession of his own mind. We know some minds which are so negative that we would not recommend that their owners take possession of them, but we would recommend that they convert them from the negative to the positive, then take possession of them. The possession of a negative mind is a costly possession. Mr. Carnegie intended to have made this clear when he admonished people to take possession of their own minds. He had reference, of course, to the potentialities of a positive mind.

Mary Baker Eddy described this same thought, in different terminology, when she said:

We know that a statement proved to be good must be correct. Now thoughts are constantly obtaining the floor. These two theories—that all is matter, or that all is Mind—will dispute the ground, until one is acknowledged the victor. Discussing his campaign, General Grant said, "I propose to fight it out on this line, if it takes all summer." Science says: All is Mind and Mind's idea. You must fight it out on this line. Matter can afford you no aid. . . . Harmony is produced by its principle, is controlled by it. Divine Principle is the Life of man. Man's happiness is not, therefore, at the disposal of physical sense. Truth is not contaminated by error. Harmony in man is as beautiful as in music, and discord as unnatural, unreal.

If I interpreted Mrs. Eddy's thought accurately, she said, substantially, that the energy of thought is good or bad, negative or positive, only because of the use one makes of it, through one's mental attitude.

There is but one kind of thought. It can be given many kinds of expression, either negative or positive. Reasoning on that simple premise, one can easily see that any negative emotion can be changed into a positive expression that may be helpful. In this possibility may one find the most profound application of enthusiasm.

The same energy that brings the pain of sorrow may be converted and made to bring the joy of creative action, in connection with one's Definite Major Purpose, or some minor purpose. Here is where self-discipline comes to one's aid. Only the disciplined mind can transmute sorrow into joy.

The art of converting negative emotion into positive expression is acquired by the formation of habits designed to coordinate the action of the mind with the action of the body. In this respect college athletics have much in their favor, for it is a well-known fact that an enthusiastic athlete may easily convert his enthusiasm from athletics to any sort of occupational endeavor he chooses.

Tennis provides the very finest of media through which habits of coordination between the mind and body may be formed, and for this reason, if for no other, tennis should become the national game for all people, both the young and the older people.

The man who has the bad habit of allowing his mind to use up energy in connection with worry will find tennis an excellent medium through which to convert his worries into enthusiastic courage. An hour on the tennis court, applied vigorously, will leave little room in one's mind for worry.

Athletic training has another benefit. It develops the habit of clean sportsmanship as well as the habit of enthusiasm. And life calls for both of these qualities if one is to enjoy the greatest measure of success.

Anything that creates temporary harmony in one's mind tends also to develop enthusiasm. The musician can exchange his worries for enthusiastic courage with the aid of his favorite musical instrument, and do it quickly. One famous author spends his "rest" time, between working spells of about one hour each, at his piano. Very often he does nothing but run the musical scales, but the coordination between his hands and his mind gives him rest and renews his energy.

As Mr. Carnegie appropriately stated, this question of coordination between the mind and the body, through some form of vigorous action, is one of the surest and quickest ways of preparing the mind for enthusiasm.

Dancing is another excellent form of exercise through which coordination between the mind and the body prepares the way for enthusiasm. I have heard an experienced teacher of dancing say that this form of exercise has been used successfully in treating patients suffering with mental disorders. The benefit comes, doubtlessly, because the rhythm of the dancing tends to clear the mind of complexes and fears, thus providing temporary expression of enthusiasm. This theory harmonizes perfectly with Mr. Carnegie's views.

The author has trained himself, over a long period of years, to think on his typewriter! The moment he touches the keys, his mind begins to function with enthusiasm, his imagination becomes more alert, and ideas begin to flow in a steady stream. On many occasions he has endeavored to think through a theme before beginning to express his thoughts in writing, only to discover that his thoughts were lacking in fluency. On some occasions he has found it necessary to begin writing, perhaps on some subject foreign to that on which he was thinking, until his mind "warmed up" and enthusiasm began to appear. On other occasions he has found it necessary to tear up the first eight or ten pages of his manuscript and rewrite it, because he lacked enthusiasm at the beginning.

This experience harmonizes perfectly with the experience of the public speaker who finds it difficult to express himself brilliantly until he "warmed up" his mind through the first five or ten minutes of his speech.

Athletes have similar experiences. That is why they go through the familiar "warming-up" process before beginning the game. They cannot play their best until there is sufficient coordination between the mind and the body to produce enthusiasm. The condition is entirely mental, not physical. Remember, therefore, that the first step one should take, in transmuting negative thought into positive action, is some form of physical action that is coordinated with one's thoughts.

WHAT ENTHUSIASM IS AND WHAT IT DOES

Let me briefly describe the more important effects of enthusiasm. Mr. Carnegie has already presented an outline of the major destroyers of this essential quality of the mind. What, then, does enthusiasm do?

1. Enthusiasm "steps up" the vibrations of thought and thereby makes the faculty of the imagination more alert.

2. It clears the mind of negative emotions and thus paves the way for the development of faith.

3. It radiates confidence and sincerity.

4. It gives a pleasing color to the tone of the voice.

5. It helps to take the drudgery out of work.

6. It adds to the attractiveness of personality.

7. It inspires self-confidence.

8. It aids in the maintenance of sound health.

9. When accompanied by appropriate physical action, enthusiasm becomes of major importance as a medium for transmuting negative emotion into positive emotion.

10. It gives the necessary force to one's desires to influence the subconscious section of the mind to act upon them promptly. It is believed by some psychologists that the subconscious mind acts only on thoughts that are emotionalized, although the emotion may be either negative or positive.

OTHER ATTRIBUTES OF ENTHUSIASM

Enthusiasm is the major factor which converts an "order taker" into a master salesman.

It takes the "dryness" out of public speech by establishing harmony between the speaker and his audience. Thus it is an indispensable quality in the work of anyone whose occupation depends, for its success, upon the spoken word. The enthusiastic speaker takes charge of his audience at will.

It gives brilliancy to the spoken word, and there is considerable ground for the belief that it may enable a speaker to avail himself, directly (through the subconscious mind), of the power of Infinite Intelligence. There is no doubt that it gives one an alert memory.

But, far and away, the two most important functions of enthusiasm are these: It definitely serves as the major factor in converting negative emotion into positive emotion, and it prepares the mind for the development of Faith! Compared with these, all other functions of enthusiasm are inconsequential.

As Mr. Carnegie has stated, enthusiasm is the result of motive! One cannot become enthusiastic without a cause. Enthusiasm, therefore, is an important factor in carrying out the object of one's Definite Major Purpose. It is no less an asset, of course, in attaining one's minor purposes.

Enthusiasm is the action factor of thought! Where it is strong enough, it literally forces one into physical action appropriate to the nature which inspired it. I believe, therefore, that Mr. Carnegie appropriately emphasized the importance of the relationship between enthusiasm and physical action.

The development of enthusiasm without appropriate physical action is something like exploding a charge of dynamite in open air, where nothing happens except a loud noise. By moving promptly, through some form of appropriate physical action, when inspired by enthusiasm, one develops the habit of enthusiasm.

A splendid way to begin this habit is by injecting enthusiasm into the spoken word. Here is a starting point within reach of everyone. It is one habit which requires no preparation to begin it. Start where you stand, and begin, now, to train yourself to speak with enthusiasm, no matter to whom you are speaking, or for what purpose. This habit will overcome timidity. It will inspire greater self-confidence. It will develop initiative. Train yourself not only to speak with enthusiasm, but to inject a pleasing tone into your voice. Loud talk, without controlled tone, may become nothing but offensive noise. Learn to dramatize words so they carry the exact meaning you intend them to carry. Nothing is more essential for success than effective speech. Speech is not effective if it is without color and enthusiasm.

You will be surprised at the improvement you can make in your speech within a single week, if you will make a studied effort to inject emotional feeling into every word you speak. Enunciate clearly. Speak each word separately; do not run your words together by speaking some of them so inaudibly they can barely be heard. Speak out clearly and distinctly, and put force behind every word! One of the common evils of most people is careless speech. Remember that your manner of speech gives others a perfect clue as to the workings of your mind and the nature of your character.

Here is one method by which you can acquire the habit of coordinating your thoughts with the physical action of speech. Within a month's time, you can so improve your manner of speech that you will hardly be recognized by your acquaintances when you speak. This habit will become one of the more beneficial media for the development of self-discipline, for obviously there is no form of self-discipline that is more essential for success than discipline over one's spoken words. Most people talk too much, talk too carelessly, and say too little that is of advantage to them. Discipline over speech will overcome this fault. Thus it will have served the double purpose of eliminating a fault and developing a virtue, through a single effort.

You can carry on your discipline over speech in all your conversations without anyone knowing that you are doing so. Begin with the members of your own family. Continue with your friends and acquaintances. Make it a part of your daily routine never to speak a single word that has not been studied and carefully modified before you speak it. Use words sparingly, as if they cost you five dollars a word. Never speak just to hear the sound of your own voice, or to impress others with your wisdom. Speak only to convey such thoughts as you wish others to receive from you, and be sure to put the exact feeling into your words that you wish the listener to interpret.

There is enough sound advice in the preceding paragraph to make the difference between success and failure for many people. It is one of the tragedies of the age in which we live that the advice is one badly needed by a majority of the people.

If it is true that "talk is cheap," it may be true because the speaker, himself, is "small." Remember this before you speak. Observe, with benefit to yourself, how sparingly successful men use words. They seldom engage in what is known as "light conversations." Profanity is not on their vocabulary list. They spend no time in idle gossip. They do no slandering of other people. When they speak, they generally say something that is worth hearing.

The man who has a steady flow of carelessly spoken words seldom has anything else! He is usually not among the successful. Time, to him, is something to be "killed," but it is nothing more. He intrudes himself into conversations without either cause or invitation, and too frequently he will monopolize the conversation. If he has enthusiasm, it is wasted because his words will have no beneficial influence with anyone.

I am emphasizing the subject of speech because speech is the major means of expressing enthusiasm! Let us not foul this great outlet for enthusiasm with "cheap talk" that has no purpose. There is no place where Definiteness of Purpose is more appropriate than it is in connection with speech. Words that have no purpose might better have been left unspoken!

The business of living, of mastering obstacles and attaining a modest degree of success, is a serious business. It requires all of one's time and effort. No one has even a minute he can afford to waste in idle talk, or careless speech.

It is no mere accident that only a few people succeed in making life pay on their own terms, while the vast majority go through life as failures. Analyze the use people make of their time, and you will observe the cause of both success and failure. Successful people work with Definiteness of Purpose and devote all their time, in a spirit of enthusiasm, to the attainment of that purpose. The failures devote their time to eating, sleeping, doing as little work as they can get by with, and purposeless talk. The difference in the ability of men is not the determining factor of their success or failure. It is the use they make of their ability that counts.

One of the strange circumstances of many who fail is the fact that if they had gone one single step further they might have succeeded instead. Every successful person I have analyzed acknowledged that he would have failed, innumerable times, if he had not kept on when overtaken by defeat. The person who is driven by an obsessional enthusiasm is not so apt to accept temporary defeat for failure. His will to win is greater than his willingness to quit. If enthusiasm did nothing else except sustain one in the times of defeat it would justify all the time that is necessary to cultivate it.

Enthusiasm is one quality that is indispensable to the man who has made up his mind to attain a high goal in life. It is the quality that helps him convert defeat into renewed effort.

I had an interview with Thomas A. Edison which disclosed the great inventor's power of enthusiasm. It also provided a significant suggestion as to the value of the Master Mind principle in the development of enthusiasm. Let us see what the great Edison had to say on this subject.

"Mr. Edison," I began, "you have given the world the talking machine, the moving picture, incandescent electric light, and a score of other useful mechanical devices, and now I have come to ask you to give to the world the secret by which you mastered discouragement and temporary defeat while you were perfecting these conveniences."

Edison made no reply. I turned red in the face, and looked around to see if anyone could explain the inventor's silence, when Mr. Meadowcroft, Edison's secretary, broke in, saying, "I'm sorry I did not tell you, but Mr. Edison is deaf. You have to write your questions on a piece of paper."

From there on, the interview moved smoothly. The question was repeated in writing and Edison began by asking, "Where shall I begin?"

"Begin with your early boyhood, if you do not mind," I replied, "and tell me about your schooling."

"Oh, my schooling, eh? Well, I suppose you know that my teacher sent me home from school after I had been in school only three months, with a note saying I did not have enough sense to take a schooling, and there is where my book learning stopped. But I guess this turn of events was fortunate, because it saved me the time that I might have spent in useless study of abstract rules and forced me to begin school in the greatest of all educational institutions, *the university of hard knocks*.

"You know that education comes from surmounting difficulties," the inventor continued, "and not from reading about them."

I asked Edison to tell the story of how Edwin C. Barnes had managed to start as a clerk in the Edison offices and lift himself to the status of a business partner. Edison grinned broadly as he began the story.

"Perhaps Ed Barnes should tell you about this himself, but I will give you a part of the story. One day I looked up from my work and saw a young man standing there, with a suitcase in his hands. Meadowcroft said the young man had arrived on a freight train, and he looked as if he had. Then Ed took over the conversation by explaining that he had come a long way to go to work for me, and he said he would start anywhere. I put him to work, but he wanted me to know that sooner or later he was going to become a business partner of mine.

"I looked him over from head to foot, very carefully. I must have embarrassed him very much, because he spoke right up and said, 'You know, I do not have to work, Mr. Edison, I could starve to death if I wanted to.' This made a hit with me, because the lad's eyes flashed with the fire of enthusiasm that marked him as one who would never quit until he got what he went after. I gave him a job, sweeping floors, and that is all I ever had a chance to give him, because *he kept me busy receiving from him after that*, until he finally gave himself a partnership with me, installing Ediphones. When you talk to Barnes, ask him about his suits of clothes. He has thirty-one of them, you know, one for each day of the month. He said he needs them to stimulate enthusiasm."

Those who believe jobs are hard to get, and complain about not having "pull" enough to get a chance at the better positions, will do well to remember how the only business partner Thomas A. Edison ever had found his chance. Certainly it was not by accepting difficulty as anything more than a stepping-stone. Certainly it was not by doing as little work as he could "get by" with.

Edison said, "I gave him a job, sweeping floors, and that is all I ever had a chance to give him." In this sentence may be found an idea of great value to all who have personal services for sale.

Pushing away from the Barnes story, I asked Mr. Edison if he had not found his deafness to be a great handicap. As quick as a blast Edison shot back this reply, "No! It is no handicap; it is a blessing— a great blessing, I might say—it saves me the annoyance of listening to a lot of useless chatter from people who have nothing to say and take plenty of time saying it. The loss of my hearing *forced me to acquire the habit of listening from within, where I found an approach to a source of knowledge from which most of my inventions came.*"

"Was it true," I asked, "that you lost your hearing as the result of a cuff on the ears by an irate conductor of a railroad who became angry because you accidentally set the baggage car on fire?"

> ✳
> *We must learn to love something*
> *outside ourselves, something greater*
> *and stronger.* — CHARLES WAGNER

"Yes," Edison replied, "that is the way it happened. Years afterward I saw the conductor and thanked him for what he did."

The interview swung back to the invention of the talking machine. "It has been said that you were several years perfecting the first talking machine. Will you state, Mr. Edison, whether this is true?"

"No," Mr. Edison replied, "I succeeded in making a piece of wax revolving on a cylinder pick up and record the words 'Mary had a little lamb' the first time I tried it."

"Will you state what gave you the idea of a talking machine? Didn't you feel that you were wasting your time?"

"Something from inside me (inspiration), something like a hunch, kept telling me to keep on trying and I would find what I was seeking. As strange as it may seem, I found the secret very close to where I began looking for it, and with the aid of the selfsame crude apparatus with which I began my experiments. For years after the first sound had been recorded and reproduced on this machine, it was used as a sort of model and all commercial talking machines were patterned after it."

"Am I to understand from your remarks, Mr. Edison," I asked, "that you believe there is a source of knowledge outside of that which is known to men through experience, and aside from that which has been recorded in books?"

"If there hadn't been such a source of knowledge," the inventor replied, "the first talking machine never would have been perfected, for you must remember *it was the first*. I had no precedent to follow. No one else had left any information on the subject to guide me. The secret of recording and reproducing the vibration of sound was literally yielded up to me from a source of knowledge not generally known to men."

"Will you state what you believe this hidden source of knowledge to be," I asked, "and is it available to all who wish to use it?"

"I have a theory about this. Perhaps it is something more than a mere theory, because I have tested it many times, but I doubt that I can describe it so you can accept it. The theory is that all knowledge exists in the form of energy, as a part of the great energy known as the ether, and this higher source can be reached only by those who have the willpower and faith to *project their conscious thoughts, through persistent concentration*, until those thoughts connect with this higher source of vibration in which all knowledge is recorded.

"You know of course," the inventor continued, "that Dr. Elmer Gates has discovered that he can sit in a dark room, with his mind concentrated on the known factors of an unfinished invention, until he forces the *unknown factors to present themselves in the form of thoughts*. He does not always succeed, but he does succeed often enough to enable him to earn his living by sitting for ideas for some of the best-known corporations. Moreover, he has completed over one hundred inventions begun by other inventors who could not quite make them work, by sitting for the answer to his demand for the unknown elements."

The inventor was becoming rather profound for a young writer, but subsequent interviews with Dr. Elmer Gates proved that Mr. Edison's statements were true. Mr. Edison said that when he found the solution to his problem, while working on the incandescent electric lamp, he did so by bringing together two old, well-known principles and coordinating them in a way never tried previously, and that the idea came to him as a "hunch" just after he had dozed off for a few minutes of sleep, after a hard day's work in search of the solution.

The principles were old, as Mr. Edison said, but the combination in which they were brought together was new. It came to Mr. Edison from that great hidden source of knowledge which he described as the source to which he always turned when organized knowledge, gained by men's experience and his own experiments, failed to yield the answer to his problems. This leads one to wonder if Mr. Edison did not come very near uncovering the source from which the needed knowledge for man's next big step upward in civilization will come. It also leads one to wonder if he did not uncover, in what he termed the "hidden source" of knowledge, something of great value to educators who are interested in helping man to *use his mind more intelligently.*

Remember, this interview took place with one of the great inventors of the world, and not with a long-haired, soapbox promulgator of ideas designed to be of help to others. I was interested in knowing how Mr. Edison managed to become a great scientist without at least an elementary knowledge of mathematics, chemistry, and physics.

"How did you manage to get by without an elementary schooling?" I asked Mr. Edison. The reply was illuminating. With a twinkle in his eyes the inventor replied, "Men with technical training can be employed. They have had plenty of elementary training, you know, but I rarely had to call upon them. The majority of my inventions were completed by the use of common horse sense, plus persistence, plus *definite knowledge of what I wanted to accomplish.* Most people do not know what they want. Schooling would do them no good, no matter how much of it they had. The biggest factor in the perfection of the talking machine was the *definite knowledge of what was wanted*. I saw that machine in my mind before I did a lick of work to create it. And what was more important, I made up my mind to make a machine record and reproduce the words "Mary had a little lamb" if it took the rest of my life to do it. There never was any doubt that I would perfect a machine that would do this, and this certainty of purpose led also to certainty of plans and persistence of effort, which are two of the essentials of success in any undertaking. If you can convey this one thought to people trying to find success, you will render them a greater service than any they can get in most schools."

The public has heard many different versions of the relationship which formerly existed between Edison, Henry Ford, Harvey S. Firestone, and John Burroughs. I asked Mr. Edison to describe the influence which bound these four men together so closely for so many years.

"Was it friendship, alone, which brought Mr. Ford, Mr. Firestone, Mr. Burroughs, and yourself together?" I asked.

"Not friendship, alone," he replied. "It was something deeper than mere friendship. We found our association provided a source of thought stimulation that was helpful to each of us. Burroughs, you know, was a thought provoker. I think that we all received useful ideas from his fertile brain.

"Wherever two or more people coordinate their minds in a spirit of harmony," Mr. Edison continued, "each person experiences a form of mind stimulation which lifts his thoughts above those of the average, workaday type of thought. This fact was responsible for the coining of the term 'roundtable,' as it is a well-known fact that whenever a group of men sit down and begin seriously and harmoniously to discuss any subject, there comes from the discussion ideas, plans, and knowledge of the subject not previously known to any person in the group."

The principle Mr. Edison was describing was the "Master Mind," through which men avail themselves of the knowledge of others without the necessity of gaining that knowledge through experiences of their own. Mr. Edison explained that he made use of this principle freely, in connection with his work as an inventor, and stated that it was through the use of this principle that he bridged the deep chasm caused by his lack of elementary schooling. Andrew Carnegie described the principle of the Master Mind as being responsible, more than all the other principles of individual achievement, for the accumulation of his great fortune, and Dr. Gates acknowledged it as the principle through which he perfected hundreds of inventions.

Mr. Edison emphasized the fact that only minds that are coordinated in a spirit of *perfect harmony* can get the full benefit of this principle. The reminder is significant. It was Mr. Edison's description of the principle of the Master Mind which inspired me to turn the spotlight of attention upon this principle so persistently that it led me to the discovery that the principle has been used, either consciously or unconsciously, *by every person who has attained outstanding success in any calling.*

Since the first interview I had with the great Edison, the maps of the world have been rewritten and the economic depression has changed the habits and the fortunes of men all over the world, but the seventeen principles of achievement, some of which Mr. Edison used, remain the same, and these are times favorable to those who understand and apply these principles.

The depression left millions of men without positions. Perhaps many of them have tried and failed several times since the depression began. To all such it will be helpful if they will remember that the great inventor of Orange, N.J., *tried and failed ten thousand times* before he perfected the incandescent electric lamp.

Some of those who lost their positions during the depression may profit by remembering the spirit of Ed Barnes, who was so determined to become the partner of Mr. Edison that he went to Orange, N.J., by freight train, and was willing to begin as a floor sweeper. *It pays now, as it paid young Barnes over thirty years ago, to know what one wants and to be willing to stand by one's plan until the end is achieved.*

Mr. Edison taught the world great lessons, not the least of them the fact that *success comes to the person who refuses to accept anything else.* Edison was in no way discouraged after failing ten thousand times. The average man would have quit at the first signs of failure, let alone at the end of ten thousand failures, which explains why there are so many "average" men and there was but one Edison.

Mr. Edison's plans often failed, just as the plans of other men failed. When one plan failed, with determination and enthusiasm he replaced it with another and kept on toward his goal, but *he did not change his goal.* After he had tried 9,999 plans, and all of these had failed, he did not say, "Oh, well, what's the use? I will change my mind and build a machine that will peel potatoes instead." He went right ahead and chose the ten thousandth plan and lo! it was the one that worked. *Edison's persistence, and his belief that out there somewhere in the cosmos may be found the answer to all problems, had projected into space the pattern of a definite idea and that idea had found contact with a physical counterpart.* By what strange alchemy this took place, no one, not even the great Edison, has ever been able to explain.

Mr. Edison believed that life was something to be seized, harnessed, and ridden. He proved that no one is ever defeated until and unless he accepts defeat as such in his own mind. His partner, Edwin C. Barnes, proved that no one, not even a poor lad without "pull" and without railroad fare, need go without a job. Moreover, he proved that no one need accept a humble job at menial labor and remain at that job longer than is necessary to merit a better one. He chose, as his major purpose in life, a partnership with the great Edison *and made his choice become a splendid reality.* Luck, chance, favorable "breaks" had nothing to do with his good fortune. It was of his own making, created in his own mind, carried out in his own mind. Not everyone can become a partner of the world's greatest men, but everyone can and should aim high, at some definite goal, and then enthusiastically put heart and soul back of that aim until all obstacles melt away or until obstacles can be transformed into stepping-stones on which one may climb nearer the object of that aim.

Mr. Edison has gone, but the simple principles that made him stand out from the crowd as the world's greatest inventor are as available today as they were when he found them and put them to work, and the greatest of these principles is *enthusiastic singleness of purpose* plus *concentration of effort on that purpose until it has been fully clothed in its physical or financial equivalent.*

All success begins in the form of an impulse of thought, an *idea!* Mr. Edison carried his ideas beyond the thought impulse stage by the simple process of placing back of them a *burning desire* (enthusiasm) for their realization. His obsession was invention, the most difficult, perhaps, and generally the least profitable of all occupations. But Mr. Edison accumulated a sizable fortune from his work, thus proving that Definiteness of Purpose, backed by enthusiasm, can create opportunity wherever one wills.

HOW TO DEVELOP THE HABIT
OF ENTHUSIASM

Enthusiasm, as the term is used in this chapter, describes the modus operandi by which the emotions of the heart and the reasoning power of the head may be combined in whatever proportion one desires.

There are certain steps one may take that will lead to the development of the habit of enthusiasm, viz.:

1. Adopt a Definite Major Purpose.

2. Back that purpose with an obsessional desire (enthusiastic motive) for its attainment.

3. Create a definite plan, or combinations of plans, and begin immediately to carry them out, keeping in mind Mr. Carnegie's emphasis on the importance of coordination between the mind and the body, through physical action.

4. Transfer both the purpose and the plan to the subconscious mind by writing them out clearly and repeating what you have written, many times daily.

5. Follow through with persistence based on all the enthusiasm you can develop, remembering that a weak plan persistently applied is better than a strong plan applied intermittently, or without enthusiasm.

6. Keep away from "joy-killers" and confirmed pessimists. Their influence is deadly. Substitute, in their place, associates who are optimistic, and above all, do not mention your plans to anyone except those who are in full sympathy with you.

7. If the nature of your Definite Major Purpose requires it, ally yourself with others whose aid you require.

8. When overtaken by defeat, study your plans carefully, and if need be change them, but do not change your purpose.

9. Never let a day pass without having devoted some time, even if it be ever so little, to carrying out your plans. Remember, you are developing the habit of enthusiasm, and habits call for physical action.

10. Autosuggestion is a powerful factor in the development of any habit. Therefore keep yourself "sold" on the belief that you will obtain the object of your Definite Major Purpose, no matter how far removed from you the object of your

purpose may be. Your own mental attitude will determine the nature of the action your subconscious mind will take in connection with your purpose. Keep your mind positive at all times, remembering that enthusiasm thrives only in a positive mind. It will not mix with fear, envy, greed, jealousy, revenge, hatred, intolerance, and procrastination. Enthusiasm thrives on action!

From here on out you are on your own!

The next move is yours, and no one can make it for you. I can tell you what you must do to enjoy the power of enthusiasm, but I cannot help you do it. No one can help you but yourself and your Master Mind allies, if you have such.

Remember Mr. Carnegie's statement that enthusiasm is contagious, but remember, also, that pessimism is contagious. Cultivate personal associates who express enthusiasm, and be sure to include at least one such person in your Master Mind group.

Every person lives in two worlds! The world of his mental attitude, which is greatly influenced by his physical environment and his personal associates, and the physical world in which he must struggle for a living. The circumstances of the physical world may be greatly shaped by the way one relates himself to his mental world. This he can control. The physical world is beyond his control, except to the extent that he attracts that portion of it which harmonizes with his mental attitude.

Enthusiasm is a great leavening force in one's mental world.

It gives power to one's purposes. It makes for harmony within one's own mind. It helps to free the mind of negative influences. It wakes up the imagination and stirs one to action in shaping the circumstances of the physical world to his own needs!

A man without enthusiasm or a Definite Major Purpose resembles a locomotive without either steam or a track on which to run, or a destination toward which to travel.

Enthusiasm is the action-producing factor of thought!

Where it is lacking, its place usually is taken by the habit of procrastination.

If you are one of the ninety-eight persons out of every one hundred who do not know what they want most, make it your business to find out what you want. Be definite in your decision.

No amount of enthusiasm can take the place of Definiteness of Major Purpose! If you do not know precisely what you demand of life, you may be sure that you will get nothing except that which life has left over, after those with a definite purpose get through choosing. The leftovers are not desirable.

If you do know what you want, go after it now! Put everything you have into your efforts. Let your desire become obsessional so it will drive you instead of your driving it.

If you are a citizen of the United States, you know that you live in a land of plenty: plenty of opportunity, plenty of material wealth; plenty of demand for people who can render useful service. If you do not fit where you are, you can change. Experience has proved, over and over again, that a man can do pretty much anything he really wishes to do.

Depressions have come and gone in the United States, many of them. Wars come and go. And men, both the successful and the unsuccessful, come and go. But the greatest nation on earth remains the land of greatest opportunity throughout all these changes. Somewhere your opportunity exists. Find it! Embrace it and make the most of it, never minding the pessimists and the never-do-wells who, because of their own failure, try to convince others that this country should be torn asunder and built over.

There is nothing wrong with this country except some of the

people. Those who sincerely seek opportunity find it. They do not find it, however, by "waiting to see what is going to happen." They find it by making something happen, right where they stand, by acting on their own initiative in a spirit of unshakable Faith in themselves and the future of their country.

There is no opportunity in this country for the person who is willing to "sell it short," by listening to defeatists and professional propagandists. This country has always reserved its greatest opportunities for those who expressed the greatest Faith in its future. It will continue to do the same.

The man who takes his cue from a soapbox rabble-rouser, and writes off his opportunity by allowing himself to be thus influenced, deserves the loss that is sure to become his. The world does not reward unbelievers. It rewards those who have Faith in Infinite Intelligence, Faith in their fellow men, and Faith in themselves. Enthusiasm inspires Faith in self. The unbroken record of individual achievement, through the opportunities provided by the American way of life, should give one Faith in the future of this country.

I call attention to this spirit of defeatism which spread in the United States after the beginning of the business depression, and especially after the beginning of the second World War, because it makes enthusiasm difficult.

Defeatism is deadly to all who embrace it at any time, but it is more dangerous in war periods than it is when the conditions of the world are normal, because in emergency periods it is spread by professionals whose only object is to destroy the American way of life. One does not have to do anything, or say anything, to help these professional propagandists. One has only to allow his Faith in his country to be undermined, his confidence in himself destroyed.

Because the habit of enthusiasm prepares the way for an abiding Faith, this principle deserves to be studied carefully and applied vigorously now, when the seeds of distrust are being so viciously sown throughout the nation.

Do not be contented with reading this chapter but appropriate its contents and put them into service, beginning with yourself and continuing by teaching others to supplant defeatism with Faith. As Mr. Carnegie has stated, one never learns anything adequately until he begins to teach it to others. Mr. Carnegie also emphasized the importance of coordination of the mind and the body, through appropriate physical action, as a practical means of developing the habit of enthusiasm.

We are living in a world that is grief stricken and mentally sick! We know that the cause of the sickness is the maladjustment in human relationships, and we know, equally well, that the philosophy of personal achievement offers the way to a better understanding. It has the answer to most of the problems that now confuse and embarrass people in every walk of life. This has been proved by the astounding record of the philosophy in the past, even before it was fully tested and prepared for the people in its present form.

> *Every great and commanding moment in the annals of the world is the triumph of enthusiasm.*

The Philosophy of American Achievement is rapidly becoming the standard guide in human relationships in almost every walk of life, among people of all races and creeds. It has found its way into the sales organizations of outstanding life insurance companies, and it is doing full-time duty, for employer and employee alike, in banks, retail stores, and industrial plants, all of whom have found in it a common meeting ground on which they can negotiate with full assurance that it will benefit alike all whom it serves.

In view of all the highly organized endeavor to "divide and control" the people of America that is going on throughout the nation, most of which is aimed at destroying the working relationship between employers and employees, it is encouraging to know that this philosophy is serving as an antidote for this un-American, destructive endeavor.

In the closing pages of his book *Adventures of a White-Collar Man*, Alfred P. Sloan, Jr., president of General Motors, gives a striking illustration of the part this sort of philosophy has played in the success of that industrial empire.

In his own terminology he describes the General Motors operating philosophy as follows:

"Management: The collective effort (Master Mind principle) of intelligence, experience and imagination.

"The facts: A constant search for the truth. (Organized thought.)

"The open mind: Policy based upon analysis without prejudice. (Liberty of thought; tolerance.)

"Courage: The willingness to take a risk, recognizing the fact that leadership exacts a price. (Organized Individual Endeavor; Applied Faith.)

"Equity: Respect for the rights of others. (The Golden Rule applied.)

"Confidence: The courage of one's convictions. (Applied Faith; self-discipline.)

"Loyalty: The willingness to make any sacrifice for the cause. (Going the Extra Mile—doing more than one is paid for.)

"Progress: There must always be a better way. (Creative vision.)

"Work: The catalyst (acceleration) that energizes all these ingredients, so that they may take their respective parts in promoting the common cause. (Organized Individual Endeavor.)"

The words in parentheses are mine, and they name the success principles Mr. Sloan was extolling, knowingly or not. Thus we see that Mr. Sloan has mentioned several of the principles of the Philosophy of American Achievement as being the foundation of the business philosophy of the great General Motors industrial organization.

"Such are the basic principles that I laid down," said Mr. Sloan, "as my platform for the guidance of the organization at the time I became president of General Motors Corporation.

"As the years have passed," he continued, "they have been my constant guide. They have never failed in the many moments of stress and doubt. I am sure they will never fail any individual or organization, irrespective of the problems or the difficulties that must be faced.

"Bill Knudsen and I were sitting in the Press Club of the General Motors Building at New York World's Fair. We had just celebrated its opening. A thousand distinguished guests had seen the exhibit and had taken a ride through the Futurama. We had had dinner. A moving picture had been shown dramatizing the recent accomplishments of American industry in the form of new things—methods, processes and products. Every individual enterprise represented, and many others as well, had contributed to a symposium of progress. It was a stupendous record of accomplishment, especially in the face of a long period of depression. Everyone was electrified by what had been seen and heard.

"I realized that, in many ways, it was a new top in our evolution. Here were shown all our products, dressed in the very latest technical mode. A great array of devices dedicated to better living, making possible a wider horizon of contact and enjoyment.

"'You know, Bill,' I said to Mr. Knudsen, 'all these products really tell the story of the American plan of free enterprise; the ceaseless research in the hope of producing more and better goods and services at ever greater values. They are symbolic of American industry today—the industrial scheme of things that is constantly turning luxuries into everyday conveniences for more people.'

"'And what we must never forget in this country,' said Knudsen, 'is that the only way to provide more jobs for people is to keep on doing the things that made all these things possible—only do them still better. Quality products, better methods, good wages, low prices, better tools, fair dealing. And,' he added, 'plenty of hard work from everybody.'

"'Just think, Bill,' I said, 'the wonder of it all is that we have only just begun. The opportunities for America are beyond the dreams of any man now alive, if we will only, through persistent work and enterprise, continue the pattern that was begun so long ago.

"'Take the Futurama, for instance—a conception of what the world of 1960 may look like. But who knows what the world of 1960 really will be like? The real world of tomorrow will outstrip anything we can imagine today, if only we in this country will keep our vision and hold our faith in the fundamentals that make for progress.

"'New comforts for the city, a new life for the country, conveniences in the home, progress in better living—new highways, new means of communication, strides in health and education and culture—the mind of man just cannot comprehend all the things that lie within our reach.'"

This philosophy will do more to antidote the vicious spirit of defeatism than anything we can imagine.

Skilled technicians and scientists are working continuously, in the research laboratories of such concerns as General Electric Company, General Motors Corporation, Ford Motor Company, and

United States Steel Corporation, where huge sums are being spent annually, in search of new and better ways of doing things. These men are not working aimlessly, with the hope of coming upon information of value, but they are searching for definite information on specific subjects. Here you will find the Philosophy of American Achievement in operation in its highest and most commendable form.

The American way of life provides an abundance of opportunity for the person who makes these success principles a part of his daily routine, and, as Mr. Sloan has so well stated, "The opportunities for America are beyond the dreams of any man now alive, if we will only, through persistent work and enterprise, continue the pattern that was begun so long ago."

He might well have added, "If we will continue the pattern that was begun so long ago, in the same spirit of enthusiasm and faith that this pattern was created by those who have gone before us."

This sentiment reminds me of a statement made by Andrew Carnegie, while he was helping me organize this philosophy, viz.:

"Never worry about the lack of opportunities in America. If you must worry, let it be in connection with the lack of ambition, the lack of enthusiasm, the lack of creative vision which are so essential in embracing opportunities.

"We have not even scratched the surface of American opportunities. The possibilities of future achievement in this country are so far ahead of past accomplishments that there is hardly room for comparison. We have more natural resources than any country in the world. We have more private wealth, per capita, than any nation in the world. We have the highest standard of living known to civilization. Yet, with all these advantages, we have just begun to make use of our opportunities. We can lead the world in industry, science, education, and culture if only we can produce enough leaders to inspire the people of America to take the fullest advantage of their privileges and opportunities!"

> ✳︎
> *Whatever a man can imagine,*
> *he can do.*

When Mr. Carnegie looked ahead into the future and made this statement, we had no radio, no great system of improved highways, no great automobile industry, no Federal Reserve Banking System, no refrigerators within the means of the humblest householder, and wages were but a fraction of what they are today. Therefore, in the light of what has happened in this country in the brief span of a little over thirty years, which has more than justified Mr. Carnegie's prophecy as to the future of America, we have sound reason for looking ahead into the future and prophesying that the accomplishments of the next thirty years will make those of the past thirty years look insignificant by comparison.

The fruits of these future accomplishments will be the work of men and women who master and apply this philosophy. Likewise, they will belong to those who have the foresight and the ambition to apply the philosophy. It has been that way in the past; it will be that way in the future. Opportunity, in a free country such as ours, belongs to the man who moves on his own initiative, in a spirit of enthusiasm, backed by Faith. Nothing can change this except the spirit of defeatism which is being infiltrated into this country by envious nations whose leaders would like to enjoy our benefits without giving anything in return for them. Personal enthusiasm, Definiteness of

Purpose, self-reliance, personal initiative, and personal ambition can kill off this spirit of defeatism.

The future of America justifies anyone in developing enthusiasm. That is why men of vision—such men as Alfred P. Sloan, Jr., and Henry Ford, and Owen D. Young, the heads of the great life insurance companies, and the builders of airplanes, such as Eddie Rickenbacher— pay no attention to the philosophy of defeatism, but go right ahead with expansion programs that demonstrate their Faith in the future of this country.

And that is why the research laboratories of the great industrial firms of America are working day and night, preparing ways and means of developing the future and helping the people to make the most of it.

The future of America, as seen through the eyes of one out-standing scientist, was briefly described a little while ago by William D. Coolidge, director of research of the General Electric Labora-tories, in these words:

"The other day a newspaper man told me that a million dollars awaits the one who discovers a swifter way to make newspaper en-gravings. I can tell you how to go about it: find a ray which, when projected through a photographic negative onto a plate, will quickly etch out the plate. But I can't tell you what ray to use, nor what plate.

"Another million should go to the man who invents a simple, cheap way to make good paper prints of color photographs.

"The word 'impossible' is to a scientist much like a spur to a horse. One of the impossibles for years was a perfect union between glass and metal, because under the influence of cold or heat they contract and expand at different rates, thus pulling them apart. But not long ago Dr. Albert Hull, of our laboratory, walked into my office with a large glass cylinder fastened tightly to a metal cylinder. He had found a combination of metals that had exactly the same contracting rate as a special glass he had developed. Now that we can marry glass and metal many articles can be made better and more cheaply.

"Recently a customer returned an electric motor because, he reproached us, 'This is wound with bare wire.' We had a hard time convincing him that the 'bare' wire was safely insulated. Nor could we blame him for being skeptical. For thirty years there had been almost no innovations in insulating wire; we had to use cumbersome cotton, or paper, varnishes and enamels which easily cracked. Only lately had we learned of an insulating substance, made from coal and lime, that we could so apply to a wire that it seemed to become a very part of it. Wire coated with it could be smashed flat or twisted thousands of times; still the coating was intact. Already this magic coating is spreading through industry.

"In 1916 America had only nineteen industrial research laboratories. Today, in nearly 2,000 laboratories, a vast treasury of ingenious brains and intricate mechanisms are hard at work on our national defense, improving the supercharging of airplane engines, developing searchlights so powerful that, by the beam of one of them, a newspaper was easily read in an airplane twelve miles from the searchlight. Other projects are too secret to mention. . . .

"Perhaps one day you will buy food in silver-plated cans. Already a scientist I know has produced some of them. We have lots of silver, which could substitute for tin in cans, a factor of vital importance to defense should our supply of tin be cut off.

"There is a shortage of well-trained organic chemists and metallurgists, and limitless opportunities in both fields. Chemists, mechanical engineers, and electrical engineers have great jobs to do. So, too, have the physicists. There is Uranium 235, the 'wonder metal,' one pound of which will give as much energy as millions of pounds of coal, when someone discovers how to separate that pound from the common variety of this element with which it is associated in nature.

"The new fluorescent light demands better materials. Television demands a more sensitive camera tube. Aviation demands a reliable way to make blind landings. And there is the old dream of harnessing sunlight. We have already used it to generate steam and small electrical currents, but perhaps someday some wonderful new material, extremely sensitive to sunlight, will fully open this magic door.

"The list is endless. Nothing is anywhere near perfect. Industry and research are crying for good men, and fame and fortune hide in every test tube, under every microscope."

Of course Dr. Coolidge was speaking of the possibilities of achievement in the world of physical things. That is his world, and it is as he suggests, richly laden with opportunities for those who specialize in it.

But there is another field which offers still greater opportunities than any that exist in material things. It consists in the possibilities of unfoldment of the mind, the exploitation of the brain, the functioning and the power of thought. Here is a world all unto itself, a world that has barely been touched by science.

Someone, perhaps many, will begin research into the operations of the mind, starting where this philosophy ends! Perhaps this field of research will disclose some method by which unjustified fears and self-imposed limitations of the mind can be removed at will.

The subconscious section of the mind is a vast, unexplored universe of available power which needs further understanding. If it is, as some believe, the only connecting link between the conscious mind and Infinite Intelligence, some method should be found by which it can be freely used by all, and not confined to the few who make a study of mind phenomena. Perhaps this is the branch of mind phenomena through which a better approach to the power of thought will be discovered.

The "sixth sense," through which so-called hunches and inspired ideas are received, should come in for exhaustive study through organized research. Here is a field that staggers the imagination of man. It may be the medium by which the individual mind can be connected at will with all the knowledge and all the facts existing in the universe, and all that have ever existed, from the beginning of time. The research should begin by a study of the media by which the subconscious mind can be stimulated to action, because the "sixth sense" obviously is closely related to the subconscious, if not a definite part of that faculty.

Where is the seat of the subconscious mind located? How can one stimulate it into action at will? What must one do to clear the way for the subconscious mind and the "sixth sense" to function? These are the questions that need to be, and perhaps they will be, answered. And they will lead us to enjoy the spiritual as well as the material benefits of life.

It is not dogma, or creed, or religion alone that I am consumed with. It is something more which I fear humanity has lost in the mad scramble for material things. I envision a future world made up of people who will practice the spirit of brotherhood instead of merely talking about it—a world in which avarice and greed and selfishness will be brands of vulgarity, a world in which men will live peacefully together, each knowing that there is plenty for all and no need for anyone to injure another in order to benefit himself, a world that may not be the so-called Utopia, but one in which common decency among men will be the order of the day, by choice and by habit!

✳

WISHES WON'T BRING
RICHES. ACTION
MUST FOLLOW
THOUGHT TO REACH
ONE'S GOAL.

✳

HATS OFF TO THE PAST; COATS OFF TO THE FUTURE.

—DAN CRAWFORD

※

WHAT IS A MAN GOOD FOR WITHOUT ENTHUSIASM?

CHAPTER THREE

✳

ORGANIZED INDIVIDUAL ENDEAVOR

I n this chapter we begin the analysis of one of the distinguishing features of successful leaders. This quality is also a distinguishing feature of Americanism, so important that it has been guaranteed to every American citizen in the Constitution of the United States.

It is the privilege of individual initiative, a quality that is no less essential in the achievement of personal success than that of Definiteness of Purpose.

Without doubt the privilege of *exercising one's own initiative* is the very last that any ambitious American would wish to give up, for it is obvious that without this privilege noteworthy achievement is an impossibility in any calling.

We, the people of the United States, have set the whole world a worthy example in the exercise of our personal initiative in the field of industry and commerce and in the professions. To this one quality, more perhaps than to any other, we owe our right to claim this to be "the richest and the freest" country of the world.

The subject of Organized Individual Endeavor, as presented in this chapter, describes the methods by which an individual may make purposeful and profitable use of his right to and responsibility for the exercise of personal initiative. No privilege is of benefit if one sleeps upon it. No privilege can be of great benefit to anyone unless it is organized into a definite plan and put into action.

In this chapter Andrew Carnegie describes the methods through which personal initiative can be *organized* and used for the attainment of definite ends. The lesson begins in Mr. Carnegie's private study, in 1908, with me as the student:

HILL:

You have stated, Mr. Carnegie, that Organized Individual Endeavor is among the most important of the principles of individual achievement. Will you analyze this principle in its relationship to personal achievement?

CARNEGIE:

Very well, let us begin by saying that personal initiative may be likened to the steam in the boiler in this respect: It is the power through which one's plans, aims, and purposes are put into action! It is the antithesis of one of the worst of all human traits, *procrastination.*

Successful men are known, always, as men of action! There can be no action without the exercise of one's initiative. There are two forms of action, namely, (1) that which one indulges in from the force of necessity and (2) that which one exercises out of choice, on his own free will. Leadership grows out of the latter. It comes as the result of action in which one engages in response to his own motives and desires.

HILL:

Would you say that the right of individual initiative is among the greatest of the privileges we enjoy as citizens of the United States?

CARNEGIE:

It is not merely among the greatest; it is the greatest! This privilege was considered of such great importance that it was specifically guaranteed in the Constitution to every citizen of the United States. The privilege of exercising one's personal initiative is of such great importance that every well-managed business recognizes and properly rewards individuals who show aptitude in the use of their own initiative for the betterment of the business.

It is through the exercise of personal initiative that the most humble worker may become an indispensable factor in any business. It is through the exercise of this privilege that the humblest day laborer may become the owner of the business in which he works.

HILL:

From what you say I take it that you believe the privilege of acting on one's own initiative is the stepping-stone of major importance in all individual achievement.

CARNEGIE:

I have never known of anyone achieving outstanding success without acting on his own initiative. Under our form of government and our industrial system every man is rewarded according to the service he renders through his own initiative. No one is forced to do anything against his will. But the American way of life is such that it encourages everyone to promote himself through his own efforts into whatever station in life he wishes. Those who organize their efforts naturally get ahead faster than those who drift, without definite aim or purpose.

HILL:

There must be certain definite characteristics of leadership which the more successful leaders develop and apply. Will you give me a catalog of such traits as you believe to be essential for leadership?

CARNEGIE:

From my own experience with men I have observed that successful leaders in all walks of life exemplify one or more of thirty or more traits of leadership, and in some instances they possess all of these traits:

1. The adoption of a Definite Major Purpose and a definite plan for attaining it.
2. The choice of a motive adequate to inspire continuous action in pursuit of the object of one's major purpose. Nothing great is ever achieved without a *definite motive*.
3. A Master Mind alliance through which to acquire the necessary power for noteworthy achievement. That which one man can accomplish by his own efforts is negligible, confined in the main to the acquisition of the bare necessities of life. Great achievement always is the result of coordination of minds working toward a definite end.
4. Self-reliance in proportion to the nature and scope of one's major purpose. No one can go very far without relying

largely upon his own efforts, his own initiative, his own judgment.

5. Self-discipline sufficient to give one mastery over both the head and the heart. The man who cannot or will not control himself never can control others. There are no exceptions to this rule. This is so important that it should probably have headed the entire list of the essentials of leadership.

6. Persistence, based on a will to win. Most men are good starters but poor finishers. The man who gives up at the first signs of opposition never goes very far in any undertaking.

7. A well-developed faculty of imagination. Able leaders must be eternally seeking new and better ways of doing things. They must be on the lookout for new ideas and new opportunities to attain the object of their labors. The man who trails along in the old path, doing things merely because others have done them, without looking for methods of improvement, never becomes a great leader.

8. The habit of making definite and prompt decisions at all times. The man who cannot or will not make up his own mind has little opportunity to induce others to follow him.

9. The habit of basing opinions on known facts instead of relying upon guesswork or hearsay evidence. Able leaders take nothing for granted without a sound reason. They make it their business to get at the facts before forming judgments.

10. The capacity to generate enthusiasm at will and direct it to a definite end. Uncontrolled enthusiasm may be as detrimental as no enthusiasm. Moreover, enthusiasm is contagious, as is also lack of enthusiasm. Followers and subordinates take on the enthusiasm of their leader.

11. A keen sense of fairness and justice under all circumstances. The habit of "playing favorites" is destructive to leadership. Men respond best to those who deal with them justly, and especially where they are dealt with fairly by men in higher positions of authority.

12. Tolerance (an open mind) on all subjects at all times. The man with a closed mind does not inspire the confidence of his associates. Without confidence great leadership is an impossibility.

13. The habit of *Going the Extra Mile*—doing more than one is paid for and doing it with a positive, agreeable "mental attitude." This habit on the part of a leader inspires unselfishness on the part of his followers or subordinates. I have never known an able leader in business or industry who did not endeavor at all times to render more service than any man under his authority.

14. Tactfulness and a keen sense of diplomacy, both in spirit and in deed. In a free democracy such as ours, men do not take kindly to brusqueness in their relationships with others.

15. The habit of *listening much and talking little*. Most people talk too much and say too little. The leader who knows his business knows the value of hearing other men's views. Perhaps we are equipped with two ears, two eyes, and only one tongue that we may hear and see twice as much as we speak.

16. An observing nature. The habit of noting small details. All business is a composite of details. The man who does not become familiar with all the details of the work for which he and his subordinates are responsible will not be a successful leader. Moreover, a knowledge of small details is essential for promotion.

17. Determination. Recognition of the fact that temporary defeat need not be accepted as permanent failure. All men occasionally meet with defeat, in one form or another. The successful leader learns from defeat, but he never uses it as an excuse for not trying again. The ability to accept and carry responsibilities is among the more profitable of accomplishments. It is the major need of all industry and business. It pays higher dividends when one assumes it without being required to do so.

18. The capacity to stand criticism without resentment. The man who "flares up" with resentment when his work is criticized will never become a successful leader. Real leaders can "take it" and they make it their business to do so. Bigness overlooks the smallness of criticism and carries on.

19. Temperance in eating, drinking, and all social habits. The man who has no control over his appetites will have very little control over other people.

20. Loyalty to all to whom loyalty is due. Loyalty begins with loyalty to one's self. It extends to one's associates in business. Disloyalty breeds contempt. No one can succeed who "bites the hand that feeds him."

21. Frankness with those who have a right to it. Subterfuge which misleads is a poor crutch to lean upon, and it is one that able leaders do not use.

22. Familiarity with the nine basic motives which actuate men. Emotion of love, emotion of sex, desire for financial gain, desire for self-preservation, desire for freedom of body and mind, desire for self-expression, desire for perpetuation of life after death, emotion of anger, and emotion of fear. The man who does not understand the natural motives to which men respond will not be a successful leader.

23. Sufficient attractiveness of personality to induce voluntary cooperation from others. Sound leadership is based upon effective salesmanship, the ability to be sympathetic and to make one's self pleasing to others.

24. The capacity to concentrate full attention on one subject at a time. The jack of all trades is seldom good at any. Concentrated effort gives one power that can be attained in no other way.

25. The habit of learning from mistakes—one's own and the mistakes of others.

26. Willingness to accept the full responsibility of the mistakes of one's subordinates without trying to "pass the buck." Nothing destroys one's capacity of leadership quicker than the habit of shifting such responsibilities to others.

27. The habit of *adequately* recognizing the merits of others, especially when they have done exceptionally good work. Men will often work harder for friendly recognition of their merits than they will for money alone. The successful leader goes out of his way to give credit to his subordinates. A pat on the back denotes confidence.

28. The habit of applying the Golden Rule principle in all human relationships. The Sermon on the Mount remains a classic for all time, as a sound rule of human relationship. It inspires cooperation that can be had in no other way.

29. A positive "mental attitude" at all times. No one likes a "grouchy," skeptical person who seems to be at outs with the world in general. Such a man will never become an able leader.

30. The habit of assuming full responsibility for each and every task one undertakes, regardless of who actually does the

work. Perhaps this quality of leadership should have headed the entire list, and it would have if the qualities of successful leadership had been listed in the order of their importance.

31. A keen sense of values. The ability to evaluate in the light of sound judgment without being guided by emotional factors. The habit of putting first things first.

All these qualities of leadership are capable of development and application by any person of average intelligence.

HILL:

From your analysis of the qualities of leadership, it appears that successful leadership is largely a state of mind or mental attitude. Is that your understanding of it?

CARNEGIE:

No. Leadership is not entirely a question of the proper mental attitude, although that is an important factor. The successful leader must possess definite knowledge of his life's purpose and work. Men do not like to follow a leader who obviously knows less about his job than they do.

HILL:

What is the best method for inspiring men to become leaders in their chosen occupations?

CARNEGIE:

Men do things because of a motive. Leadership can best be inspired by planting in a man's mind a definite motive that forces him to acquire the qualities of leadership. The profit motive is one of the most popular. When men make up their minds to acquire wealth or attain success, they usually begin to exercise their privileges of personal initiative along lines that develop leadership.

HILL:

Then you believe it would be inadvisable to discourage the desire for personal wealth?

CARNEGIE:

Let me answer you in this way: This country is recognized the world over as having more leaders in industry and business than any other nation. These leaders developed their qualities of leadership in response to their desire for wealth. Obviously anything which kills off this desire would strike at the very roots of our national resources, *a major portion of which consists of the creative ability of the men who manage industry.*

HILL:

Would you say that the desire for private riches is the only motive that has inspired so many Americans to develop the qualities of leadership?

CARNEGIE:

Oh no! Not by any means. We have many able leaders in America whose major motive is that of building and creating. The pride of personal achievement is a strong factor in the American way of life. Beyond the point at which a man acquires economic security, he begins to become motivated largely by his pride of achievement. One man can eat only one meal at a time, wear one suit of clothes at a time, and sleep in one bed. After he acquires security in connection with these necessities, he begins to think in terms of desire for public acclaim. He wishes to become recognized as a successful person. There may be a few men with the hoarding instinct of the miser; but a majority of the successful men of America think in terms of the use they can make of money instead of endeavoring to accumulate money for the sake of having it. It has been this desire for self-expression, through the use of money, that has made America the great industrial nation that it is.

HILL:

From what you have said, I take it that the possession of great riches by one individual may be either a blessing or a curse, according to the use he makes of his riches. Is that your viewpoint?

CARNEGIE:

That is my belief, precisely. Take John D. Rockefeller as an example. He has accumulated a vast fortune, but every dollar of it is at work, developing, extending, expanding some form of useful industrial, business, or philanthropic service. Through the use of his money, he provides employment to many thousands of men. But it serves a still higher purpose. Through the Rockefeller Foundation the Rockefeller fortune is serving mankind in scores of ways that have nothing whatsoever to do with further profits for Mr. Rockefeller. His fortune is fighting disease and helping to suppress the enemies of mankind in other ways. It is helping to uncover useful knowledge through scientific research, the benefits of which will extend to generations yet unborn.

HILL:

Then you would say that the people of America are better off because of the manner in which Mr. Rockefeller has exercised his personal initiative in the accumulation of riches?

CARNEGIE:

Not only the people of the United States, but the people of the entire world are benefiting by his initiative and his acquisitive spirit. What this country needs is not fewer men like Mr. Rockefeller, but more of his type. Take James J. Hill as another example. Through his personal initiative, he built the great transcontinental railway system that opened up millions of acres of unused lands and brought the Atlantic and the Pacific Oceans within easily accessible proximity to each other. It would be difficult to estimate the wealth which—by the exercise of his personal initiative—this one man has added to the riches of America. It probably amounts to billions of dollars. The private fortune he accumulated for his services is as nothing compared to the wealth his activities added to the nation as a whole.

HILL:

You might include yourself in that category also, Mr. Carnegie. Would you mind estimating the wealth your own personal initiative has added to the country?

CARNEGIE:

I much prefer to speak of the achievements of others who have done more than I. But if you insist on an answer, let me call your attention to the impetus that has been given to the building of skyscrapers since my associates uncovered more economical and better methods of producing steel. You know, of course, that the modern skyscraper would be an impossibility without the use of the steel frame. The skyscraper would also be an economic impossibility if steel were as expensive as it was when I entered the business of manufacturing steel. We have given the country a better product than any it knew before we entered the business of making steel and we have brought prices down to where steel can be substituted for the less satisfactory products of wood and other metals of less durability. When I first entered the steel business, steel—such as it was—sold for around $130 per ton. We brought it down to around twenty dollars per ton. Moreover, we so improved the quality that steel now serves scores of uses for which it was not suited until we improved it.

HILL:

Was your major motive that of making money, Mr. Carnegie?

CARNEGIE:

No, my major motive always has been that of making men more useful to themselves and to others! As you may have heard, I have had the privilege of making millionaires of more than forty men, most of them men who began working with me as ordinary laborers. But the money these men accumulated is not the important thing I wish to stress. In helping them to accumulate money, I helped them to become a great asset to this nation. By inspiring them to exercise their own initiative, I started them to rendering useful service that has contributed richly to the development of the great industrial system of America. You see, therefore, that these men became more than owners of riches; they became intelligent users of riches, and as such they provided employment for many thousands of men.

Wealth consists in material things and human experience properly mixed. The more important part of the mixture is brains, experience, personal initiative, and the desire to build and create. Without these qualities money would be useless. Understand this truth and you will have a better knowledge of the nature of our American riches. We are a rich nation because we have a great number of pioneers whose pride of personal achievement has enticed them to exercise their right of individual initiative in all forms of business and industrial activity.

These men may think they were motivated by the desire for personal riches, but the truth is that they were influenced by the much greater desire for personal achievement. Regardless of the motives by which they were actuated, they have helped to convert a vast wilderness into the world's richest and most progressive nation. This could not have been accomplished without the free, voluntary exercise of the personal initiative of the men who did the job.

HILL:

What part has the American form of government served in the development of American industry, Mr. Carnegie?

CARNEGIE:

A very necessary part, indeed. If you will read the Declaration of Independence and the Constitution of the United States, you will see clearly that the men who wrote those profound documents clearly intended to surround the people of America with every conceivable right and opportunity for the free exercise of personal initiative. Under no other form of government do men receive such definite encouragement to exercise their personal initiative.

HILL:

Then you see no reason for changing our form of government?

CARNEGIE:

Not unless we find still better ways of influencing men to take possession of their own minds and use their abilities on their own initiative. Our form of government is not perfect, but it is the best the world has yet discovered. It provides far greater liberties and privileges for the use of personal initiative than the majority of men are using intelligently. Why change it until the people of America catch up with it by using the opportunities it provides? Tinkering with things that serve satisfactorily is one trait that gets men into difficulty. This is one form of personal initiative that should be discouraged. It comes under the heading of "meddlesome curiosity." If a man has good health he should go about his business and not interfere with nature by experimenting with cures of diseases with which he does not suffer. However, there are some who do not follow this rule. They are known as hypochondriacs, and they are always suffering with imaginary illness. We are in a healthy economic condition in this country. We have vastly greater undeveloped resources than any we are using. Let us not experiment with our economic system, but rather let us make more intelligent use of our present system, to the end that we may make better uses of our great resources.

Nations that are always experimenting with their systems of government and their economic systems are engaged in revolutions and counterrevolutions most of their time. No small part of our success here in America is due to the spirit of harmonious relationship existing between the states of the Union. That harmony is the direct result of our form of government which wisely provides an incentive for harmony among the people. In union there is strength. This is true of business and industrial groups the same as it is in the relationship between the states.

HILL:

What do you believe to be the greatest possible evil that might curtail the success of the American people as a whole?

CARNEGIE:

Anything that would, in any way, weaken the spirit of harmony between the people. Our unity of purpose is our greatest national asset. It is vastly more important than all our natural resources, for without this we would become the victims of any greedy nation that might wish to take our natural resources away from us.

We fought a tragic war among our own people to maintain our national unity. While memories of this war linger in the minds of some, now we all recognize that a separation of the states would have meant the beginning of our disintegration. And I might well add that the greatest evil that can overtake an industry or a business is that which disturbs the harmonious working relationship between those engaged in it. Business succeeds through the friendly cooperation of those engaged in it. Personal initiative is a power for good only when men combine their experience and ability and work toward a common end in a spirit of harmony and understanding.

HILL:

Then you do not look with favor on those who make it their business to stir up strife, hatred, and envy among men who are engaged in the operation of the American industrial system?

CARNEGIE:

No, this is a form of personal initiative which may help some; but it destroys the rights of many. In our own industry I have never had any misunderstanding with those who work for me except that which was inspired by professional agitators who profit by disturbing human relationships. That is the worst of all forms of personal initiative. How could I have had any misunderstanding with men who, down to the humblest worker, knew that the door of opportunity was wide open day and night to those who wished to earn more by making themselves worth more? The man who helps wage earners to rise from day labor to become millionaires, as I have done whenever I had the opportunity, is not likely to have any misunderstanding with his men if he is left alone to deal with them on the basis of free enterprise.

HILL:

But, Mr. Carnegie, are there not some employers who do not take such a constructive attitude regarding their relationship with their employees? Are there not some employers who greedily clamor for more than their share of what their business produces?

CARNEGIE:

Yes, there are some such. There always have been. There will always be men of greed. But they do not last. Competition soon eliminates them. That is one of the benefits of the system of free enterprise under which we operate in America. Here an employer must make good or make room, and he cannot make good at the expense of his employees. His competitors see to that!

HILL:

When and under what circumstances should one begin to exercise personal initiative?

CARNEGIE:

The time to begin using personal initiative is immediately following one's definite decision as to what one wishes to accomplish. The time to begin is right then. The place to begin is right where one stands. The time to act is now. Lay out a plan for acquiring your goal, prepare to give an equivalent value for it, and begin then and there to put the plan into action. If the plan chosen turns out to be weak, it can be changed for a better one; but any sort of plan is better than procrastination. The universal evil of the world is procrastination—the terrible habit people have of waiting for the time to begin something to be "just right." It causes more failures than all the weak plans of the world.

HILL:

But shouldn't one consult others and get their opinions before beginning important plans?

CARNEGIE:

Now listen here, young fellow! "Opinions" are like the sands of the desert, and most of them are about as slippery. Everyone has an opinion about practically everything, but most of them are unworthy of trust. The man who hesitates because he wants the opinions of others before he begins to exercise his personal initiative usually winds up by doing nothing. Of course there are exceptions to this rule. There are times when the counsel and advice of others are absolutely essential for success; but if you refer to idle opinions of bystanders, let them alone. Avoid them as you would an epidemic of disease, for that is exactly what idle opinions are—a disease! Everyone has a flock of them, and most people hand them out freely, without being asked.

If you want an opinion on which you can rely, consult the man who is known to be an authority on the subject in connection with which you seek an opinion. Pay him for his counsel, but avoid "free opinions" because they are generally worth exactly what one pays for them.

I recall, quite clearly, what some acquaintances of mine said when they heard I was planning to cut the price of steel to twenty dollars a ton. "He'll go broke!" they shouted. They gave me free advice without my seeking it. I passed it by, and went ahead with my plans. Steel came down to twenty dollars a ton.

When Henry Ford announced he would give the people a dependable automobile for less than a thousand dollars, they shouted, "He'll go broke!"; but Ford went ahead with his plans, and one day he will be the dominating factor in one of America's greatest industries. *And he'll not go broke!*

When Columbus announced that he would sail his little boats across an uncharted ocean and discover a new route to India, the Doubting Thomases cried out, "He's crazy! He'll never come back." But he did come back.

When Copernicus announced he had invented an instrument with which he had revealed hidden worlds never before seen by the human eye, these same "free opinion" fellows hooted, "Heretic! Put him to the torch!" They actually wanted to burn him for daring to use his own initiative.

When Alexander Graham Bell announced he had invented a telephone with which people could talk to one another at long distance, by the use of wires, the unbelievers yelled, "Poor Alex has gone crazy!" But Bell went ahead with his idea and perfected it, although the time did not appear to be "just right."

And you'll have your turn with these "free opinion" boys who spend their time trying to discourage men from using their own initiative. You'll hear them cry out, "He can't do it! He can't give the world a philosophy of individual achievement because no one has ever done it before." But, if you take my advice, you will go right ahead and back your judgment on your own initiative. When you succeed, as succeed you will, the world will crown you with glory and lay its treasures at your feet; but not until you have taken the risk and have proved your ideas sound. Don't become discouraged because other people may tell you "the time is not right." The time is always right for the man who knows what he wants and goes to work to get it. The world needs a philosophy of individual achievement. It has always needed such a philosophy. Go ahead and supply that need, no matter how long it takes, or what sacrifices you may have to make to do the job. Do the job the best you can and you'll learn, from firsthand experience, that these calamity howlers are nothing but a bunch of disappointed human beings who are suffering with an inferiority complex because they have neglected to use their own initiative.

HILL:

That was quite a speech, Mr. Carnegie, and I take it for granted that you meant it mostly for me.

CARNEGIE:

Yes, I meant it for you, and through your efforts I hope it will serve the yet unborn generations, long after I shall have passed on. The world needs men who have the courage to act on their own initiative. Moreover, men of this type write their own price tag and the world willingly pays it. The world willingly rewards men of initiative.

The privilege of personal initiative is an important part of the American way of life, but the privilege is worth nothing if it is not exercised. What we need most here in the United States is a continuous sales campaign for the sole purpose of keeping the American people inspired with a desire to take advantage of the opportunities available for the accumulation of riches. The government should conduct a continuous campaign designed entirely to bring to the attention of the people the nature and scope of the opportunities available to them.

HILL:

Then you believe there are still enough opportunities for individual success, in the United States, to go around to all the people?

CARNEGIE:

Yes, there is an opportunity to match the *ambition and the ability* of every person in the United States. But opportunity will not hunt the man. The order must be reversed through Organized Individual Endeavor. The greatest opportunities will be available to those who are the most capable of organizing and directing their own efforts.

HILL:

Some may not understand what is meant by the term Organized Individual Endeavor. Would you define your understanding of this principle?

CARNEGIE:

The principle of Organized Individual Endeavor consists of a very definite procedure through which an individual may promote himself into whatever station he desires or acquire whatever material things he wishes. The steps to be taken are these:

1. Choice of a definite purpose or objective.
2. Creation of a plan for the attainment of the objective.
3. Continuous action in carrying out the plan.
4. Alliance with those who will cooperate in carrying out the plan.
5. Moving, at all times, on one's own initiative.

Organized Individual Endeavor might be briefly described as *planned action*. Any action based on a definite plan has a better chance of success than effort of an unorganized, haphazard nature, such as that in which the majority of people engage. Able leadership, without Organized Individual Endeavor, is an impossibility. The two major points of difference between a leader and a follower are these: (1) the leader carefully plans his efforts, and (2) he moves on his own initiative, without being told to do so.

If you wish to find a potential leader, look around until you find a man who makes his own decisions, plans his own work, and carries out his plans on his own initiative. In such a man you will see the major requirements for leadership. This is the type of man who pioneered in American industry, and to him we owe the credit for the great American industrial system which is the envy of the world.

HILL:

But what about the quality of genius? Aren't the leaders in industry and business blessed with some form of genius which most people do not possess, Mr. Carnegie?

CARNEGIE:

Now you are talking about a fallacy that has deceived more people than any other mistaken idea. The word "genius" is badly overworked. It is generally used to explain successful achievement because most people do not take the time to dig in and find out how men succeed. Personally I do not know what a genius is. I have never seen one! But I have seen many successful men who are called geniuses. Analysis of the cause of their success would show that they are only average men who have discovered and applied certain rules which enabled them to get from where they started to where they wished to go.

Every normal person has within him the potentiality of that which we call "genius," in one field of endeavor or another, depending upon the individual's preferences, his inborn traits of character, and his ambition. I would say that the nearest quality to genius that I could describe is an obsessional desire to do some one thing and do it well, plus the willingness to act on one's own initiative. From this point on, genius is only a matter of *Organized Individual Endeavor persistently carried out.*

The man who knows precisely what he wants and is determined to get it is about the nearest approach to that which some call "genius" that I can think of. Such a man has better than an average chance of success, and when he achieves success the world is apt to look at him in the hour of his triumph and attribute his achievements to what they believe to be genius.

HILL:

But, Mr. Carnegie, doesn't the question of education enter into one's personal achievements? Isn't it true that the educated man has a better chance of success than the man who lacks education?

CARNEGIE:

That depends, altogether, on what you mean by the term "education." There is no doubt that an educated man has a better chance of success than one who is not educated. But let us define the word "educate." The word means to develop the mind from within, to educe, to draw out, to expand. It does not mean, as is popularly believed, the mere accumulation of facts. Many men are schooled, but few men are educated. An educated man is one who has learned how to use his mind so that he can get everything he desires without violating the rights of others. Education, therefore, comes from experience and use of the mind, and not merely from the acquisition of knowledge. Knowledge is of no value unless and until it is expressed in some form of useful service. Here is where the subject of personal initiative begins to prove its importance as an essential of success.

To answer your question more specifically, an educated man has a better chance of success than one who is not educated only in the event that he applies his education in the achievement of some definite objective. All too often men rely upon their possession of knowledge to take the place of Organized Individual Endeavor. They expect to be paid for that which they know instead of that which they do with their knowledge. This point is important. I have heard it said that some successful businessmen hesitate to employ men who have just graduated from college, for the reason that many college graduates "have too much they must unlearn" before they become useful in the practical affairs of business. Speaking for myself, I would much prefer a college-trained man for positions of responsibility, but I prefer them to come to me with an open mind, seeking more knowledge. I prefer those who have a sound knowledge of fundamentals rather than the tricks of the trade. I prefer those who know the difference between theory and practice.

There is one great advantage that most college graduates have over those who lack this training, and it is the fact that college training helps one to organize his knowledge. Disorganized knowledge is of very little value.

HILL:

Do you believe that alertness in the application of individual initiative is an inborn trait? That one has it, or doesn't have it, according to the nature of his hereditary gifts?

CARNEGIE:

My observation of people has forced me to the conclusion that personal initiative is largely based on personal desires and ambitions. The man who appears to have no individual initiative awakens and moves under his own initiative in a hurry when he becomes obsessed with some definite strong desire or purpose.

HILL:

Would you say, then, that personal desire is the beginning of all individual achievements?

CARNEGIE:

Yes, without a doubt! Definiteness of Purpose is the result of desire. When a man's desires take on the proportion of an obsession, he usually begins to translate them into their physical equivalent through Definiteness of Purpose. Desire, therefore, is the starting point of all individual accomplishments. As far as I know, there is no impelling motive other than desire which inspires a man to move on his own initiative. Herein lies the secret of the influence some wives have over their husbands. When a man's wife desires riches or success, she may transplant that desire in the mind of her husband and cause him to move on it in a way that will enable him to succeed. I have often known of this happening. But, in the last analysis, the desire for riches or success must become a definite motive on the part of the husband. The presence of a deeply seated desire in a man's mind has a tendency to stir him into action as nothing else can do.

HILL:

Then you believe it is true, as one philosopher expressed it, that men's faults consist in low aim and not in the stars?

CARNEGIE:

There is nothing that will take the place of high aim! When a man sets his mind upon the achievement of a definite purpose, the powers of the universe appear to be on his side. He begins to make use of every available means to attain the object of his desires. The first thing that comes to his aid is his right to the exercise of individual initiative. Personal desires can be attained only by the exercise of personal initiative. If initiative takes on the form of Organized Individual Endeavor, one's chances of success are greatly multiplied.

When you analyze individual achievement in this manner, you learn quickly enough that no great achievement is possible without the application of Organized Individual Endeavor. The use of this principle for the attainment of one's desires is not optional. *It is imperative!*

HILL:

From your analysis of Organized Individual Endeavor, I assume that this principle can be applied by the man with little schooling as well as by the man with extensive schooling; that it is not essentially a part of one's education in the popular interpretation of the meaning of the word "education."

CARNEGIE:

Lest you become confused on this point, let me make it clear that no man is educated, in the true meaning of that term, until he acquires a practical working knowledge of the principle of Organized Individual Endeavor. Moving in an orderly, well-organized manner toward a definite end is precisely the procedure of an educated person. Go back to the definition of the word "education" and study it carefully. You will observe that the application of education leaves no alternative other than that of action based on Organized Individual Endeavor. You might properly say that *Organized Individual Endeavor is education.*

HILL:

From your remarks I reach the conclusion that the so-called self-made man is an individual who has learned how to organize his efforts and direct them to a definite end.

CARNEGIE:

Yes, that describes the self-made man very well. You could have added the word *persistence* to your description, for it is a well-known fact that self-made men have the quality of persistence. In fact, all successful men carry out their plans with persistence. Without this quality, the principle of Organized Individual Endeavor may not bring success.

HILL:

It would be correct, then, to say that "success is attained by Definiteness of Purpose expressed through the persistent application of Organized Individual Endeavor"?

CARNEGIE:

That is the idea exactly! Moreover, if you analyze the meaning carefully, you will find nothing whatsoever about genius being essential for success. Almost anyone can make up his mind what he wants, create a plan for acquiring it, and proceed on his own initiative to carry out the plan. The only "genius" associated with this procedure is the necessary persistence to insure continuous action in carrying out the plan. If one is motivated by a desire which assumes the proportion of an obsession, the important factor of persistence is not difficult to acquire.

HILL:

Mr. Carnegie, you have used the word "obsession" quite frequently. Will you explain the nature of what you call an "obsessional desire"? Is this a state of mind?

CARNEGIE:

Yes, an obsessional desire is a state of mind, and it is associated with the dominating thoughts of the mind. You might say that an obsessional desire is a form of self-hypnosis in that it occupies one's mind a major portion of his time. Successful men have the habit of focusing their attention upon the ways and means of achieving the object of their major purpose so continuously that this habit becomes a form of self-hypnosis. This habit develops self-reliance, initiative, imagination, and enthusiasm, and leads to action based on Organized Individual Endeavor.

Obsessional desire has the effect of transferring to the subconscious mind a clear, definite picture of that which one wants. Through some power which science has not as yet isolated, and no one understands, the subconscious mind goes to work on such pictures by inspiring one with new ideas and practical plans for the realization of desires.

HILL:

You would say, then, that self-hypnosis is not a dangerous habit?

CARNEGIE:

The answer to that depends entirely upon the subject in connection with which self-hypnosis is practiced. I have known men who hypnotized themselves with the acceptance of poverty and failure and defeat. I have known others who hypnotized themselves with an obsessional desire for constructive achievement. I think I can safely say that no man has ever achieved great success without having been motivated by an obsessional desire that assumed the proportion of self-hypnosis.

Here let me call your attention to the fact that there is a strange unknown power connected with hypnosis which enables those under its influence to perform seemingly impossible feats. When under the influence of hypnosis, a man can lift a weight he could not even budge in his normal state of mind.

There are some forms of disease which yield readily to treatment under hypnosis. There are physicians who specialize in the treatment of certain mental disorders through the application of hypnotism. Their method of treatment is known as "suggestive therapeutics." It often serves to eliminate disease where nothing else will. Psychoanalysis is a method of psychotherapy resting on the theory (and it seems more than a mere theory) that abnormal mental reactions are due to repression of desires consciously rejected, but subconsciously persistent.

One cannot dismiss the subject of hypnosis as being a mere superstition or a power to be feared. Our fears of the subject grow out of our ignorance of its nature and its possibilities for good. We should at least have no fear of self-hypnosis when it is applied to the achievement of worthy ends, and we need not know its complete nature or purpose in order to make helpful use of it.

I am very glad you brought up the subject of self-hypnosis; for you have given me an opportunity to express what I hope may be helpful suggestions in connection with its use. Names we give to things often frighten people. This is true of the word "hypnosis." Some people are afraid of it because they associate it with "black magic" and the work of charlatans who have used hypnotism as a means of taking advantage of people. Let me offer this one word of encouragement concerning the power of hypnotism: No person can hypnotize another against his will. All hypnotism is, in the final analysis, self-hypnosis. It is a state of mind which can be produced only with the cooperation of the individual who is hypnotized.

I know a man who is the recognized leader of a great industry. He founded the industry and he has grown wealthy through its successful operation. Knowing this man as well as I do, I would say that if anyone offered to hypnotize him he would be highly insulted. He might even become frightened at the very mention of the word "hypnotism." Yet I am prepared to tell you that his success is the result of self-hypnosis! He has been hypnotizing himself through his obsessional desires in connection with his business, without knowing what he was doing. The same could be said of other successful men. Disabuse your mind, therefore, of any feeling that self-hypnosis associated with constructive, obsessional desire is dangerous. The very opposite is true!

We speak of autosuggestion without associating with it any feeling of fear. As a matter of fact, we accept the principle of autosuggestion as an essential for successful achievement. The principle of autosuggestion (suggestions we make to ourselves) is nothing but a mild form of self-hypnosis. Again let me say that we become confused too often by the names we give to things.

Doubtlessly it would be a great surprise to men who suffer poverty and failure all their lives, if they were told that their circumstances were self-imposed, through the principle of self-hypnosis, but that would be near the truth. A man can hypnotize himself with fears and self-established limitations as easily as he can hypnotize himself with obsessional desires for achievement. The subconscious mind accepts and acts upon the food with which it is fed. It goes to work on thoughts of poverty as quickly and as effectively as it accepts and acts upon thoughts of opulence. Let us not wave these truths aside as being unworthy of consideration merely because we may not understand them.

HILL:

It is your opinion, then, that both poverty and riches are a reflection of the individual's state of mind; that neither is the result of accident, luck, or other causes outside the control of the individual. Is that correct?

CARNEGIE:

That states my belief perfectly. It is not a popular belief, because those who fail to acquire riches have the bad habit of looking everywhere except the right place for the cause of their failure. Many blame our economic system for their poverty, although this country is known the world over as "the land of opportunity," and our form of government, our economic system, our American way of life are the envy of the rest of the world.

The man who cannot accumulate riches in the United States could not accumulate them anywhere else, and for the reason that our entire setup is one which encourages individual accumulation of riches. The real cause of individual poverty in the United States is the failure of the individual to grasp the fundamental principles by which riches are acquired. Too many of our people are looking for handouts. They do not recognize the fact that there is no such reality as *something for nothing*; that riches begin in the form of a state of mind based on Definiteness of Purpose plus a willingness to give something of value in return for riches.

HILL:

Of course you recognize that not all riches possessed by the American people are the result of a state of mind, and not all riches were earned by some of the people who possess them. Take, for example, the inherited fortunes. They came into possession of those who have them without anything of value being given in return, and without any relationship to the owners' state of mind.

CARNEGIE:

I can see that you have not thought such circumstances through with sufficient accuracy. While it is true that inherited riches are not earned by those who possess them, and the riches have no relationship to the owners' state of mind, you must remember that this does not apply to those from whom the riches were inherited. Somebody (perhaps with a few rare exceptions) gave something of value in return for those riches, and their accumulation was very definitely related to the state of mind of the one who acquired them.

There is another important fact in connection with inherited riches which I fear you have overlooked. Riches acquired in this manner soon go back into general distribution. That old saying that it takes only three generations for people to pass "from shirtsleeves to shirtsleeves" is quite appropriate. Inherited fortunes seldom remain in the hands of heirs for more than two generations. Our entire economic system is so arranged that it absorbs unearned riches very quickly.

There is another important fact in connection with inherited riches. Such riches usually soften those who receive them and destroy their ability to retain the riches. Here, again, we have evidence that anything one acquires without giving something of equal value in return for it has a queer way of melting away. This applies to inherited riches, to money acquired by unlawful methods, and to all forms of ill-gotten gain. Moreover, this truth is known throughout the world. It appears that the whole universe is so planned that natural law frowns upon idleness, an empty head, and the desire to get something for nothing. This fact is significant if one will only take the time to analyze it.

HILL:

Please understand, Mr. Carnegie, that I am not trying to make out a case in favor of those who seek something for nothing, or who inherit riches. I am merely trying to establish proof of the existence of an eternal justice that places everyone, as you have said, substantially where his own state of mind entitles him to be. Do you recognize the existence of such a system of universal justice?

CARNEGIE:

Yes, I do recognize the existence of such a system. Every person who gives serious thought to cause and effect recognizes it. Emerson described it convincingly in his classic essay on compensation.

There is a law of Compensation through the operation of which every man may benefit if he adapts himself to the law. It does not favor any attempt to get something for nothing. It pays no premiums on idleness or indolence. And I specifically call your attention to the fact that under our American way of life, our industrial system, our economic system as a whole, and our form of government come as near to conforming to the law of Compensation as it is humanly possible to make them. Let us see in what manner this is true.

First, the entire American way of life is designed to give every man all the liberty and freedom he will appropriate and use so long as it is not attained at the expense of another. This privilege is guaranteed to every man by our form of government, a system of government which was created with that privilege as its major purpose.

Second, our industrial and economic systems are so arranged that individuals who exercise their privilege of personal initiative, by Going the Extra Mile, are rewarded in proportion to the quality and quantity of service they render. Thus, under our system, every individual is given an adequate motive for adapting himself to the law of Compensation.

Third, our system is so arranged that our natural resources remain always available (not controlled or owned by the government or any individual or small group of individuals), and the right of free enterprise, which remains always open and available to the people as a whole, *insures* such a general and frequent exchange of our various forms of riches that everyone has an opportunity to acquire a portion of them. Our system provides for a continuous turnover of capital and commodities and all other kinds of riches. In the process of this turnover, every individual who has something of value (in services or otherwise) to give may receive his just portion of the profits connected with the turnover. In the United States one has not only that privilege, which he may exercise through his own personal initiative, but our entire American way of life beckons to him as a customer, and makes it attractive and profitable for him to take for himself as much as he can justly earn. We do not frown upon men who, by their superior skill, education, and experience, so adapt themselves to the law of Compensation that they accumulate great riches. Our system encourages men to acquire everything for which they are prepared to give something of an equivalent value.

Thus you see that the American way of life was patterned to harmonize with one of nature's most inexorable laws. In this respect the American way of life reflects the great wisdom of the men who patterned it.

Any weaknesses we find in the American way of life are weaknesses of individuals who refuse or neglect to adapt themselves to its multiple advantages, and not weaknesses of the system. There is no escape from this conclusion.

HILL:

Your logic seems to be irrefutable, Mr. Carnegie. How did you arrive at your conclusions concerning the wisdom with which the pattern makers of the American way of life arranged our system to harmonize with the law of Compensation?

CARNEGIE:

I was forced to this conclusion by observing the effects of the system in the practical affairs of industry and business. By comparing the American way of life with that of other countries, I had no choice but to recognize that ours is vastly superior to any other. Our standard of living is higher than that existing anywhere else. The opportunities for individual accumulation of riches are more extensive and varied here than in any other country. Our whole scheme of living is such that even a humble rail-splitter, born in poverty and illiteracy, may aspire to the highest office within the gift of the people and get it. In no other country now existing, or that has ever been known to civilization, has such an opportunity been available to the people.

HILL:

I assume, from all you have said, that you hold no brief for the man who complains that he has no chance to get ahead in this country?

CARNEGIE:

No, I hold no brief for such a man, but I do have a feeling of deep sorrow for all who are so ill informed as not to recognize that we are blessed with more benefits than any other people of the world. Ignorance is our greatest sin! It is my greatest hope that I may help to wipe out certain prominent kinds of ignorance in the United States by making books generally available, and specifically by giving the people a sound philosophy of individual achievement. I wish everyone to have plenty. I wish everyone to have a just share of the great riches of this country. But I know that riches can be of enduring value only to those who learn how to acquire them through their own initiative. Earned riches carry with them a certain amount of wisdom in the use of riches which is never known to the person who inherits riches, or acquires them in violation of the law of Compensation.

HILL:

You believe, I assume from your analysis, that the only sort of gift that may do no damage is the gift of practical knowledge?

CARNEGIE:

There are three types of gifts which are safe. One is the gift of knowledge or the means to acquire it. Another is the sort with which every American citizen has been abundantly blessed, the gift of opportunity to share in the benefits available in the richest country in the world, through the exercise of the privilege of personal initiative and the right of free enterprise. These are priceless gifts, and they are of a nature that can do no harm. The third is the gift of inspiration or "the will to win," which is of course essential to initiative.

HILL:

Do you believe, Mr. Carnegie, that gifts of money from parents to their children are helpful?

CARNEGIE:

The answer to your question depends entirely upon the circumstances of the gift, the amount, and for what purpose the money is intended. It is the duty of parents to give their children an adequate education. All gifts of money beyond this requirement may be, and often they are, more harmful than beneficial. You may safely assume that any gift of any nature, to anyone, at any time, which has the effect of destroying an individual's desire to earn money through his own initiative, is definitely harmful.

It is unfair to children for their parents to destroy their desire for personal achievement by gifts of money which make it unnecessary for them to prepare themselves to earn their own money. Parents who wish to dispose of money through gifts would be much wiser if they donated it to some charitable cause rather than giving it to their own children.

HILL:

What about gifts of money from a husband to his wife? Is this sort of gift advisable, and if so, to what extent should such gifts be made?

CARNEGIE:

Here, again, the answer depends entirely upon the circumstances of the gift. In the first place, you must remember that husband and wife are partners, and as such the money provided for the wife by the husband does not always come under the heading of a gift. It is generally an equitable distribution of jointly earned and jointly owned money. In many instances the wife aids the husband very materially in the accumulation of his money, and therefore has a right to share it. However, there are circumstances under which the marital relationship is damaged by too much liberality. This tendency sometimes leads to the "spendthrift" habit which may lead to financial embarrassment of both the wife and the husband. Under other circumstances, unrestrained liberality develops vanity and idleness on the part of the wife. Likewise, where the husband withholds from the wife a reasonable share of his income, his action may create resentment and lead to misunderstandings.

There is no fixed rule that will cover all marriage relationships with reference to the manner in which the husband and the wife share the income. This is something that must be settled by the application of that most uncommon thing called "common sense."

HILL:

What about gifts from an employer to his employees? Is there any safe rule by which such gifts may be made without damage to anyone?

CARNEGIE:

Some of my fellow workers have received as much as a million dollars in one year in the form of bonuses, over and above their regular salaries. This money was not a gift. It was compensation for services rendered beyond the amount of service these associates agreed to render in return for their salaries. You might say it was pay for their having gone the extra mile. Every man working with me is given an equal right to render that sort of service, and every man who exercises this right is compensated according to the value of the service he renders. The only thing that is really given, therefore, is an opportunity which is equally available to all.

HILL:

Then you do not believe in indiscriminate gifts to employees merely because an employer has converted his experience and intelligence into profits through the exercise of his own initiative?

CARNEGIE:

No, I do not believe in indiscriminate gifts to anyone, for any cause whatsoever, with the exception of donations to charity, for the benefit of those who are unable to earn money for themselves.

Let me give you an example of what may happen through gifts that have no relationship to individual equities in the gift, upon the part of those receiving it. An acquaintance of mine who is the owner of a very prosperous business decided, at the end of a very successful year, to distribute fifty percent of his profits to his employees. He gave the money to them in equal amounts, regardless of the quality or the quantity of service each employee had rendered. Three months later he was waited upon by a committee representing his employees, which demanded that he raise everyone's wages. Upon his refusal the whole group walked out on a strike which cost him all his profits for the entire year, and many thousands of dollars in addition.

You see, human nature is a queer sort of thing. His employees "reasoned" that if he could make them a voluntary gift which they had not earned, he must be making so much money that he could afford to raise their wages. It is both unsound and unsafe for anyone to give money that does not carry with it some sort of challenge and obligation. If this employer had known as much about human nature before he made the unconditional gift to his employees as he learned about it afterward, he would have distributed the money under some sort of an understanding which would have obligated his employees to give something, if nothing more than a promise to render better service than they had been accustomed to rendering.

You see from what I have said that the person who accepts something for nothing may be damaged as much as, or more than, the person from whom he receives the gift. It is always safer to give favors than to receive them, for the receiver of unearned gifts thereby places himself under obligations that may prove to be costly, to say nothing of cultivating the desire for something for nothing.

HILL:

Mr. Carnegie, are your ideas concerning human relationships shared generally by the leaders of industry?

CARNEGIE:

Yes, I think they are. You see, leadership calls for many qualities of character, some of which I have described. Among those is that of a well-developed sense of *observation of details*.

To be an able leader one must know how to negotiate with others with a minimum amount of friction. One must also know how to distinguish between human faults and virtues. These are basic requirements for leadership. Therefore, it is safe to assume that any leader of men would know, for example, that unearned gifts may do more harm than good. Also, an able leader knows that the most important link that connects him with his followers is that through which he inspires them to act on their own initiative. An able leader knows how to multiply his own capacity by inspiring others to act on their own initiative. In this manner a leader may be at many places at one time; he may do many things at the same time and do all of them well.

Take the leader of a large industry, such as the United States Steel Corporation, for example. Where would he be and what would he do if he did not know how to delegate responsibilities to subordinates with full assurance that his plans would be carried out the same as if he personally attended to the details? He would be sunk before he started!

While we are on this subject I wish to emphasize, again, the importance of one's being able to get others to use their initiative to the fullest. It was this ability, more than any other, that enabled Charlie Schwab to become so indispensable to me. It would be no exaggeration of the facts if I said that his large income was his reward for his ability to get others to do things as well as or better than he could have done them himself. Let me emphasize one idea: Men in the higher brackets of income are paid for that which they can get others to do; not merely for what they know, or what they can do individually. I doubt that there is a man living who is worth a million dollars a year if he were paid only for that which he can do individually.

HILL:

It is generally known that you have helped many of your employees to promote themselves from positions of ordinary day laborers into positions of great responsibility from which they became very wealthy. Will you describe the qualities of major importance which these men possessed that caused you to recognize them so generously?

CARNEGIE:

There was no particular generosity connected with any promotions I have made among my associates. Such promotions as were made came through the efforts of the men themselves. I had very little to do with it. But, to answer your question frankly and directly, I will name the qualities through which my associates promoted themselves:

1. The unvarying habit of Going the Extra Mile without being requested to do so. *I can say truthfully that this habit was the quality that first attracted my attention to every man I ever recognized through promotion.* I can go still stronger by saying that without this quality, a majority of those whom I have helped to become wealthy would still be performing ordinary manual labor, right where they started. It has always been one of my ironclad rules never to lift a man into a higher position or pay him more than the usual wage scale for his services unless and until he deserves recognition by voluntarily Going the Extra Mile.

2. Proven ability to accept responsibilities and discharge them with a minimum of supervision.

3. Well-established ability to induce others to use their own initiative, through the delegation of responsibilities. As I have stated, I would prefer a man who can get others to do things, and do them well, to one who has only the ability to do good work individually.

4. Loyalty to associates! A disloyal man is a poor bargain at any price. He is not only a poor investment from the viewpoint of the service he performs, which generally is little enough, but he is a great liability in connection with his

influence on those around him. One disloyal man in an organization of a thousand men will make his disloyalty felt and expressed throughout the organization.

5. A positive "mental attitude." A man with a negative mind will, likewise, discolor the minds of all with whom he comes into contact. Therefore he is also a poor bargain at any price. One thing that is essential for success in any business is harmony among those who do the work. There can be no harmony under the influence of men who carry chips on their shoulders.

6. A natural willingness to work! There is no function, no matter how great, that can take the place of work. I can say truthfully that every man who has ever held any sort of supervisory position in my organization worked harder than any man under his supervision. The man who tries to shift all his work to others will never be an able leader in any calling, no matter how much he may know, or what other qualities he may possess.

7. Persistence! The man who is a good starter, but a poor finisher, does not possess the necessary qualifications for leadership.

8. Preparation! The man who "guesses" instead of knowing will not make an able leader.

9. Definiteness of Purpose! The man who cannot make up his mind what he wants and stand by his decision does not possess the qualifications of leadership.

Here you have the nine qualities which, more than all others, have enabled my associates to promote themselves into positions of indispensability. If you analyze any successful leader I believe you would find that he has these same qualities in some measure. Naturally those who are more proficient in these qualities become the ablest leaders. Of course these are only a few of the qualities desirable for leadership, but they are the "musts" without which no one will become a noteworthy leader.

HILL:

You have said something about the habit of exercising personal initiative. Is this not one of the "musts" of the leadership list?

CARNEGIE:

Yes, and it belongs near the head of the list, but you must remember that the man who has the habit of Going the Extra Mile naturally acts on his own initiative. I did not mention this quality because it is a part of the working equipment of all who do more than they are paid for. Unless they act on their own initiative, without being requested to do so, it may be assumed that they are weak on personal initiative.

HILL:

What about honesty? Can a great leader be dishonest and get along on his other qualities?

CARNEGIE:

No one who is dishonest can be "great" at anything; least of all can he be a great leader. But you will find that if a man is loyal to his associate workers, he is more than apt to be honest in other ways. Loyalty, you know, is one of the highest and most commendable forms of honesty. A dishonest man will not by nature go the extra mile.

I am delighted that you have asked all these questions, for you have given me an opportunity to set you right on questions which others may wish answered in detail. I also like your questions because they are intelligent questions; and I like them because they show that you have a keen sense of understanding of the importance of accuracy in details. This, too, is an essential of leadership. The man who knows how to ask intelligent questions will, more than likely, know what to do with intelligent answers. I have often said that it is a greater achievement to be able to ask intelligent questions than it is to be able to answer them. You may be interested in knowing that one of the tests by which I judge men is that of their ability to ask intelligent questions. All of which I have stated, not to flatter you, but to help you emphasize the important factors of the philosophy of individual achievement.

HILL:

Will you name what you consider to be the more detrimental weaknesses of men who aspire to leadership in business and industry?

CARNEGIE:

Yes, in one short sentence: *Lack of the nine qualities I have just described!* If these are the nine most important qualities of leadership, naturally the absence of these qualities constitutes the greatest handicap to those who wish to be leaders.

HILL:

Of course! How silly it was of me to ask such a question, the answer to which should have been obvious! Well, then, let me have another try. Have you ever made the mistake of choosing men for leadership, believing them to possess the nine "musts" for leadership, but found later that they lacked some of these qualities?

CARNEGIE:

With all due modesty I can say that I have made this mistake very rarely, and for the simple reason that the men who became leaders in my organization promoted themselves into leadership by proving that they possessed these qualities prior to their promotion. You see, that is one of the great advantages of the habit of Going the Extra Mile. This habit gives a man an opportunity to bring himself to the favorable attention of his superiors while he is occupying even the humblest of positions. In the process of Going the Extra Mile a man has an opportunity to display samples of all his goods, so to speak, including whatever ability he may have in connection with the nine "musts."

HILL:

Mr. Carnegie, wouldn't it be a wise thing if the man who wishes to promote himself made a list of the nine "musts" and placed it before him where he could see it every day?

CARNEGIE:

That would be an excellent plan! It would have the effect of making one "leadership conscious." As a matter of fact, the man who aspires to leadership would do well to copy the entire list of the thirty-one qualities of leadership I have mentioned, and keep that before him constantly. At least six of the men who became members of my Master Mind group practiced that habit religiously. One of them went so far as to have the entire list cast in a bronze plaque and placed above his desk. He seldom received a visitor in his office without calling this plaque to his attention, and he invariably brought it to the attention of associate subordinates who came to his office. In this manner he discovered a great many men who later promoted themselves into higher positions.

HILL:

What other qualities of leadership are there that you have not mentioned?

CARNEGIE:

I have overlooked the most important of all. *It is the alertness of mind with which a man can recognize ability in others.* A man who can quickly recognize ability in others usually has other qualities that are essential for leadership. If you asked me what I believe my greatest asset to be I would answer, without hesitation, "The ability to pick men." Without this quality, the United States Steel Corporation never would have been born, for the corporation's greatest asset is its army of skilled men, many of whom I discovered and helped to develop. I say this with all due modesty, because it is a fact as well known to others as to myself.

HILL:

From all you have said I see that Organized Individual Endeavor consists of many different qualities, each of which plays its definite part in individual achievement.

CARNEGIE:

That is correct. You might say that the thirty-one qualities of leadership serve, as do the links of a chain, to make up the whole. Each quality serves as definite and essential a part of

Organized Individual Endeavor as the individual links of a chain serve to form a completed chain. Not one of these qualities can be omitted without weakening the whole structure of Organized Individual Endeavor.

HILL:

How may one go about developing these thirty-one qualities?

CARNEGIE:

In the same manner that any other trait of character is developed—by constant application of the qualities plus the will to excel. You must remember that all these qualities are developed by a desire for their expression. They are not inborn qualities. They come, if at all, as the result of deliberate development through use.

HILL:

Then it is possible for any ordinary person to acquire these qualities?

CARNEGIE:

Yes, anyone who is willing to work may develop them. They are not qualities to be found in the man who is *looking for something for nothing.*

HILL:

Are the qualities of leadership adaptable to one sort of endeavor the same as to others? For example, could you have succeeded as well in some other business as you have in the steel industry?

CARNEGIE:

The answer to that question would require a long explanation. However, you may be interested in knowing that I know less about the technical process of making steel than any one of a hundred or more men who work for me. The Master Mind principle provides one with a method of bridging his own deficiencies of knowledge. In my Master Mind group I have associates who know all that has been discovered, up to the present time, about the making and the marketing of steel and its related products.

To answer your question as directly as it is possible for me to do so, I will say that I probably could have succeeded as well in any other business as I have in the steel industry, because whatever business I might have entered I would have mastered through the selection of Master Mind allies who knew that business from stem to stern.

HILL:

That is precisely the information I wanted. Then I assume, from your reply, that the rules of success are universally applicable to all fields of endeavor. When a man masters these principles of individual achievement, he can apply them in any undertaking he pleases. Is that correct?

CARNEGIE:

Yes, as far as you have gone your idea is correct; but you should remember that certain men are more suited for some types of work than they are for others. In a general way a man will succeed best in the work which he likes best. Where a man is doing that which he likes to do, he will put his heart into his work. The pride of achievement enters into a man's work when he is doing what he likes best. You may put it down as a dependable fact that the man who receives no pay for his work other than that which comes in his pay envelope is being cheated, no matter how much money he receives.

The best part of a man's pay is that which comes in the form of the satisfaction he gets from doing his work well. The pride of achievement is one form of pay of which no man should deprive himself. *It is one of the tragedies of life that not every person can do the sort of work he would like best to do.* If you doubt that this is true, consider the pleasure a man gets from all forms of labor of love, such as the rendering of service for the benefit of his loved ones. When a man is motivated by a desire to render useful service to others without direct compensation, he looks upon labor as a privilege, not as a burden. From this known human characteristic, I reach the conclusion that men are always more efficient when they are doing the sort of work they like best.

To answer your question more directly, I would say that the rules of success are the same in all forms of endeavor. Moreover, these rules are as universal as are the letters of the alphabet with which one may form all the words in the English language.

HILL:

Why, then, if the rules of individual achievement are applicable to all fields of endeavor, are these rules not taught in the public schools? Would it not save many people from failure if they learned the rules of success the same as they learn the rules of mathematics or English?

CARNEGIE:

I have asked that same question, myself. I believe I can give you the answer. The rules of individual achievement have never been taught in the public schools for the simple reason that they have never been organized into a practical philosophy. I had this very possibility in mind when I assigned to you the job of organizing all the rules of achievement and all the causes of failure into a dependable philosophy. After your work has been completed, it will find its way into the public schools. The advancement of civilization *requires* this. There is no sound reason why children should spend all their school days storing up academic knowledge without acquiring also the practical knowledge of harmonious human relationship, which is one of the first essentials of success. All children should be taught, in the public schools, how to negotiate their way through life with a minimum of friction in their relationships with others.

This sort of knowledge is even more important than memorizing the names and dates of history, or as important as learning the correct usage of the English language, as important as those subjects are. Remember this one fact: Before the public schools recognize the importance of the philosophy of individual achievement it will have to be popularized through adult usage to the extent that the public schools will be forced, by public demand, to teach it. Unfortunately the public school system undergoes change very slowly, but the school system, like all other American institutions that serve the public, must take soundings of public demands and render service accordingly. Herein lies the hope that the philosophy of individual achievement will become the property of the public schools in due time.

HILL:

Mr. Carnegie, you said that the right time to begin a thing is when one makes up his mind to do it. Now there must be some plan by which the public schools can be influenced to begin teaching the Philosophy of American Achievement as soon as it has been published in textbook form. Therefore, I would like to know how you would go about introducing the philosophy in the public schools.

CARNEGIE:

You have asked me to plan a job that will require many years for its completion, and many steps will have to be taken by you before the job is finished. Speaking in general terms, here is about the way you should proceed:

First, you will have to publish the philosophy in popular textbook style and introduce it through individuals who desire to get ahead by the application of definite rules. If you are fortunate enough to find a publisher who will push the sale of your books, you will be able to do a pretty good job of distribution within from three to five years.

Second, you should begin training lecturers who will be able to teach the philosophy, so that when the time comes you can supply the public schools with teachers. Meanwhile, before the public schools are ready for them, these lecturers can make a good living, and better, by organizing private classes.

Third, you should organize your own private school for the purpose of teaching the philosophy by the home study method, thereby placing yourself in a position to reach men and women in all parts of the country who want the philosophy.

Fourth, you should have your publisher arrange for the translation of the philosophy into foreign languages, so it will be available to the mixed population of the United States who do not speak the English language. They need such a lesson in Americanism. This plan will also provide you with the means of spreading the philosophy in foreign countries.

By the time you will have taken these steps, the general public will have become so success philosophy "conscious" that the public schools will become attracted to it. The time required to bring all this about may be as much as ten years, depending, of course, upon what sort of a leader you prove yourself to be.

HILL:

In other words, it is up to me to put into practice that which I am offering to teach others. Is that the idea, Mr. Carnegie?

CARNEGIE:

That is exactly the idea! You wouldn't think much of a doctor who refused to take his own medicine if he were ill. You must become your own best advertisement of the Philosophy of American Achievement by demonstrating that you can make it work for you.

HILL:

Do you mean that I must convert the philosophy into great riches to prove its soundness?

CARNEGIE:

It altogether depends upon what you mean by the term "riches." There are many forms of riches, you know. As far as the accumulation of money is concerned, you can acquire all of that which you need, and much more, by applying the philosophy. But I wish to call your attention to a form of riches available to you which transcends, by far, any that money represents. The riches I have in mind are so stupendous in both quality and quantity that you may be surprised when I describe them. You may be still more surprised when I tell you that the riches I have in mind will not accrue to you alone, but they will become the property of the people of the world. If you recognize the far-flung possibilities of the picture I am about to draw for you, and follow the suggestions I offer, you may see the day when your riches will be vastly greater than any I possess.

THE STEEL MASTER'S CHALLENGE
TO HIS PROTÉGÉ

So, here is the picture. I warn you, before I describe it, that it will put you on the spot where your own qualifications as a leader will be shown up for precisely what they are. But I will also be on the spot, for I selected you, out of all the men I know, as the man most capable of taking the Philosophy of American Achievement to the people.

First: By the time you will have absorbed all the knowledge I shall pass on to you in connection with the philosophy of success which I have gathered from experience, you will be in possession of the greater portion of my riches. Add to this the value of the riches you will acquire from other successful men with whom I will arrange for their collaboration with you in the organization of the philosophy, and you will be in possession of the greater portion of the real riches represented by the American system. The sum total of these riches will be too fabulous for estimation, because they will be of such a nature that they may add to the riches of all the people of the United States, to say nothing of the people of other nations.

Second: You will have demonstrated the soundness of the principle of Going the Extra Mile by forcing the world to recognize you as the organizer of the first practical philosophy of individual achievement, an honor which is unusual, for no one before you has ever attempted to provide the people with such a philosophy, although the need for it has always existed.

Third: The time will come when the unity of purpose of the American people will be disturbed because of the infiltration of ideas which do not harmonize with the American way of life, and the people will be prepared, through causes beyond your control, for a dependable philosophy through which harmony may be restored. At this point the Wheel of Fortune will turn up your number, and your big opportunity will have come. You will not have to induce people to accept the philosophy. They will do that voluntarily!

I can see this opportunity already in the making. The seed of it may be found in the growing spirit of greed through which men endeavor to get *something for nothing*. The seed is gaining ground in the disturbing elements which have begun to threaten the harmony between industry and its workers. Subversive philosophies will find a convenient soil for the germination of this seed, in the labor organizations. Here is where the discord will first become obvious.

Professional agitators will work their way into the labor organizations and use them as a means of undermining American industry. The disturbance may result in some form of revolution that will strike at the very roots of the foundation stones of Americanism, but it will run its course and the American people will recover from the shock.

The people will begin to search for a way out, as the American people always do when overtaken by an emergency. Then your big opportunity will have arrived! The period of reconstruction of the American way of life will have begun, and the philosophy you will have organized by Going the Extra Mile will become, of necessity, the means by which harmony will be restored.

If you fail to see this picture as I have painted it, your failure will be mine also, because I have chosen you as my emissary to carry out the greatest assignment I have ever given to any man. If you do your work as I believe you can do it, the whole world will be richer because of your labor—richer not only in material things, *but richer in spiritual understanding*, without which no form of riches can long endure.

I hope you have recognized the fact that the Philosophy of American Achievement embodies not only the rules of material success, but also the principles expounded by the Master, in the Sermon on the Mount, "Whatsoever ye would that men should do unto you, do ye also unto them."

Unless you comprehend this broader meaning of the philosophy, you will miss the greater possibilities of your mission. The people of the world are becoming spiritually bankrupt. They are turning away from the principles of religion to embrace the principles of paganism. They can be led back to the true principles of civilization by converting their greatest weakness into an irresistible power of attraction. That weakness is their desire for material things.

Very well, the Philosophy of American Achievement provides the only known safe road to the accumulation of material riches. But it also provides the means of spiritual recovery. Therefore, in giving the people that which they desire most, you will bestow along with it *that which they need most*! Surely you will not miss this point.

Thus, in the picture I have drawn for you, you have a clear description of an opportunity such as no other American has ever possessed. This is an opportunity which may make you a great servant of the American people. Now, I have a parting word of advice: Acquire humility of the heart. Do not become overimpressed with your own importance. Accept your mission as a privilege for which to be thankful, and not as an advantage of which to boast. Remember, always, that "the Greatest Among You Shall Be the Servant of All."

. . .

Editorial Note: This advice from America's recognized leader of industry was given to his emissary, to whom he assigned the task of organizing the Philosophy of American Achievement, more than thirty years ago. It has been followed to the letter, and today we have conclusive evidence that Mr. Carnegie's prophecy as to what would happen in America was astoundingly accurate.

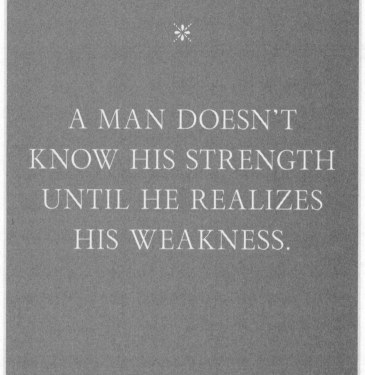

A MAN DOESN'T
KNOW HIS STRENGTH
UNTIL HE REALIZES
HIS WEAKNESS.

ANALYSIS OF CHAPTER THREE

By Napoleon Hill

In this chapter Mr. Carnegie has analyzed the "action" feature of the Philosophy of American Achievement, consisting of the thirty-one qualities of leadership.

No philosophy can be helpful until it is expressed in terms of Organized Individual Endeavor, through intelligently directed action. Therefore, this chapter may rightfully be called the dynamo that starts the wheels of individual initiative into motion.

There has never been a time during the entire history of the United States when individual initiative was more necessary than it is at the present. And there has never been a time when intelligently directed personal initiative offered greater opportunities for self-promotion than it provides at this time!

The person who combines the principle of Organized Individual Endeavor with the habit of Going the Extra Mile, and applies the combination intelligently, will be blessed with greater opportunities for self-advancement than any which have been available in the past. The two principles are closely related. When combined and properly directed, they will provide more personal power than the average man requires for the attainment of his major purpose in life.

Fortunately, we still have the privilege of acting on our individual initiative in the United States. It is one of our greatest privileges because it is by the exercise of this privilege that every man can choose his own calling, determine what sort of service he will deliver through that calling, and thereby fix his own compensation.

If Mr. Carnegie has emphasized one thought above all others in this chapter, it is the fact that all promotion is self-promotion, and it is attained through personal initiative. If the right to move on one's own initiative were denied him, he would lose one of the most important of the privileges available through the American way of life.

During the first World War and the prolonged business depression which grew out of that war, we learned that there is something infinitely worse than being forced to work. It is the unhappy circumstance of being forced not to work. As Mr. Carnegie has so appropriately stated, there is nothing that can take the place of work.

The most profitable work is that which one does on his own initiative, without force, by applying the principle of Organized Individual Endeavor. It is this sort of work to which this analysis will be devoted. I approach the analysis with full recognition that I am dealing with the very heart of this philosophy. Without a thorough understanding of the nature and importance of the principle of Organized Individual Endeavor, the students of the philosophy may not hope to benefit by it in the manner and to the extent that Andrew Carnegie had in mind.

HOW THE PRINCIPLE OF ORGANIZED INDIVIDUAL ENDEAVOR IS APPLIED

The best evidence of the soundness of a principle, as Mr. Carnegie has so forcefully stated, is that provided by the practical experience of successful men. Let us, therefore, examine the manner in which Organized Individual Endeavor has been applied in a variety of fields of endeavor associated with the American way of life.

Take the modern industrial corporation, for example, and observe how it functions successfully through the leadership of men who understand and apply the principle of Organized Individual Endeavor.

The modern corporation is nothing but a limited partnership, toward whose common operating capital the separate partners (called shareholders) have contributed in proportion to their holdings of shares. The corporation is simply a partnership made up of mechanics, farmers, merchants, clergymen, schoolteachers, doctors, lawyers, and other workmen who have invested their savings in its shares.

In addition to the operating capital required to carry on the business of a corporation, there is another asset of equal importance in the form of other partners who carry on the production activity, many of whom are also owners of shares in the corporation. These workers are divided into two classes, the workers and those who, because of their training and experience and natural aptitudes, supervise and direct the efforts of the workers.

All this activity is conducted according to definite plans which fix each worker's duties and establish each worker's responsibilities, through a highly efficient form of Organized Individual Endeavor.

If the management and labor work together in a spirit of harmony, the business thrives. Thus, working together, these partners earn the profits with which to pay the wages of the workers, with something left over to pay the partners who supplied the working capital for the use of their money, provided that no unexpected emergency overtakes the business, such as a prolonged business depression.

In such emergencies the workers receive their pay first, and the partners who supply the working capital get nothing, if the emergencies cut so deeply into the profits that the business loses money or merely breaks even.

Here we have an example of the absolute necessity for the application of the principle of Organized Individual Endeavor. The organized feature of the example consists largely of the relationship between the management and the workers. If they cooperate in a spirit of harmony, the business usually succeeds. Success is impossible without this harmonious cooperation. If the management is negligent and permits the workers to render a poor quality or an insufficient quantity of work, all the partners suffer a loss—the workers losing their jobs and the partners losing their investments.

The United States Army and Navy are excellent examples of efficient Organized Individual Endeavor. Here every man, from the highest officer to the humblest private, understands and respects the principle of coordination of effort. The crux of this form of Organized Individual Endeavor is strict discipline. If individuals disciplined themselves as definitely as do the men who manage the Army and Navy, and respected the principle of Organized Individual Endeavor as thoroughly, they would meet with fewer failures in private life.

I often wonder whether it wouldn't be an excellent form of training if every young man were required to serve a few years in either the Army or the Navy, before entering his chosen occupation, in order that he might learn at first hand the benefits of discipline based on the requirements of Organized Individual Endeavor. Certainly it would be helpful if all who aspire to leadership in any calling would take a course on leadership from men who are masters of discipline, through Organized Individual Endeavor, as are the men of the Army and Navy.

The banking business is another example of highly efficient Organized Individual Endeavor. Here, again, we find discipline from within. The great reforms in banking have always come from within the ranks of the bankers themselves. Measure bankers by the thirty-one qualities of leadership, and see how well they measure up in the application of these principles. In the field of banking there is keen competition without animosity. They have a job to do, and they do it well. As a whole, the bankers are men of fine character. They are intelligent and industrious. The rules of their profession require that they be firm in the application of definite principles, but this constraint works out to an advantage to those whom they serve the same as to themselves.

Let us take another example of the application of Organized Individual Endeavor that has led to the creation of the world's greatest nation. I have reference to the American form of government. Here we find Organized Individual Endeavor in its most powerful form. The power is provided by the people themselves. It is applied through the coordination of state and federal governments, which work harmoniously for a common purpose.

Combine this example of Organized Individual Endeavor with those previously mentioned and you have the real source of American riches and freedom. The riches exist, mainly, in the activities of industry, and banking. The freedom exists in the government. When these units of power and riches work harmoniously, the people are prosperous. When they do not work in harmony, the people suffer through business depressions, unemployment, strikes, and other disasters.

Now let us analyze another very large and important group of people who likewise constitute a part of the American way of life. Unfortunately, as a rule they do not benefit by the principle of Organized Individual Endeavor. We have reference to the American farmers. With all due respect for these fine citizens (who feed most of us), we must admit that a great many of them do not conduct their business in an organized manner. This fact is so well known that I need offer no supporting evidence of its existence.

The farmers are frequently in financial difficulty. Most of them make very little more than a living. Some of them make less. There is no escape from the fact that if the farmers operated their business under the principle of Organized Individual Endeavor, as efficiently as do the bankers and American industry, they would earn more profits and be as well off as any other group of American citizens.

From these facts we may conclude that failure to apply the principle of Organized Individual Endeavor leads to ruin, no matter whether those who neglect to apply it are individuals or groups of individuals.

Now let us dig into the farmer's habits and see wherein he fails to apply recognized rules of sound business as they are applied by industry and banking. As long as I have singled out the farmers for this frank analysis of their shortcomings, let me assist them by offering them a partial catalog of their inefficiencies:

1. The average farmer owns a farm of let us say 160 acres. Perhaps as much as fifty acres of this land he devotes to agriculture. The other 110 acres are left idle, although he pays taxes on the entire acreage. By comparison, this is about the same as if General Motors built a factory covering five acres of space, equipped it with machinery at heavy expense, but made use of only about one-third of the plant, allowing the remainder to stand idle.

2. Although scientific agriculture requires that the farmer rotate his crops for the good of his soil, the average farmer goes right on from year to year, sapping his soil with the same sort of crops.

3. The average farmer raises whatever crops his fancy may dictate, without planning his crops in accordance with market demands, thereby often producing unusable products, too much of one thing, too little of another.

4. The average farmer sells his crops in a haphazard manner for whatever he can get, whereas the businessman who operates his business under the principle of Organized Individual Endeavor has definite rules of merchandising, both in his buying and selling.

Before anyone may hope to achieve success, he must know what are his faults and learn how they may be corrected. With this fact in mind I shall play no favorites, but will describe some of the weaknesses of people as I have found them.

The list is a long one and it is authentic because it was compiled impersonally, by a professional analyst, after careful analysis of more than twenty-five thousand men and women in all walks of American life. Study the list carefully and you will understand why ninety-eight out of every one hundred people in the United States (adults) are properly classified as "failures" although we live in "the richest and the freest" country of the world, where every person has the right to exercise his own initiative; choose his own vocation, business, or trade; and live his own life as he pleases, provided he does not injure or live at the expense of others.

Self-examination is a preliminary necessity for self-promotion. Moreover, it is the only way one can carry out that age-old admonition of the philosophers, "Man, know thyself." Therefore, check yourself courageously by this list of human faults so you may lay your finger on those which are standing between you and the principle of Organized Individual Endeavor, remembering, as you do so, that every fault listed is the result of habits which may be corrected at will.

One of the great tragedies of life is the fact that we all have habits which we do not recognize as standing in the way of our success. The tragedy consists mainly in the fact that we refuse to examine ourselves searchingly. It is hoped that every person who has the ambition and the desire to get ahead through the aid of this philosophy of individual achievement will also possess the courage to take a look at himself through his own eyes without trying to cover up what he sees by excuses and alibis!

So, here is the catalog of faults which serve as enemies of Organized Individual Endeavor:

1. The *habit of trying to get something for nothing.* This habit is usually expressed through gambling, by expecting a full day's pay for a poor day's work, cheating at trade, demanding government subsidies, depending on relatives for support instead of working, and exploiting helpless human beings by group force designed to take what is wanted by force of numbers, through the expediency of sabotage and the boycott. (This habit has been placed at the head of the list, because it is so widespread that it threatens total destruction of the American way of life.)

2. The habit of neglecting, or refusing willfully, to Go the Extra Mile.

3. The habit of spending more than is earned, and failure to set up a personal budget designed to increase income by a frugal use of one's time. Individuals can no more succeed without a "balanced budget" than can governments or corporations.

4. The habit of neglecting or refusing outright to cooperate with associates in a spirit of harmony, thereby diminishing one's earning power.

5. The habit of duplicating mistakes without learning from them.

6. The habit of "guessing" instead of knowing, and of expressing "opinions" on subjects about which one knows little or nothing.

7. The habit of indulging in controversies over trivialities, thereby creating enemies needlessly, and inviting unnecessary opposition from others.

8. The habit of resorting to subterfuge instead of courageously facing the facts and realities of life.

9. The habit of drifting aimlessly, without Definiteness of Purpose.

10. The habit of working without prearranged plans that have been tested for soundness.

11. The habit of following a vocation or field of endeavor without adequate preparation.

12. The habit of scattering one's efforts without concentration of thought, purpose, and action.

13. The habit of intemperance in eating, drinking, and sex, resulting in ill health.

14. The habit of creating excuses as a substitute for satisfactory performance to cover up indifference, lack of ambition, and plain laziness.

15. The habit of allowing the emotions to run wild, without any effort to control them. The worst expression of this fault is that of giving free rein to so-called temper.

16. The habit of working as a "lone wolf" without recognizing and using the principles of the Master Mind.

17. The habit of neglecting small details in connection with one's occupation and the source of one's income and in human relationships generally.

18. The habit of acting on impulse before analysis through meditation and thought.

19. The habit of fear, based mainly on the lack of self-discipline and Faith.

20. The habit of intolerance, mainly in connection with religion, politics, and economic relationships.

21. The habit of despising ideals and other spiritual values, due mainly to greed and the love of material things. This habit has become so widespread that it has led virtually to spiritual bankruptcy in America.

22. The habit of substituting wishing for working. Wishes won't bring riches!

23. The habit of quitting when opposition appears instead of fighting on, with persistence.

24. The habit of intentional dishonesty.

25. The habit of refusing to accept gracefully the forced changes of life over which one has no control, not recognizing that the only permanent thing in the universe is eternal change.

26. The habit of neglecting to take possession of one's mind and thinking things through.

27. The habit of envying those who have succeeded instead of emulating them.

28. The habit of neglecting to "close the door" behind personal grievances, thus living in the past instead of using the present intelligently and looking to the future hopefully.

29. The habit of hypochondria (suffering with imaginary illnesses). This habit is generally the result of the desire to get out of work or a bid for sympathy.

30. The habit of trying to "keep up with the Joneses" instead of living one's own life according to one's income and social standing.

31. The habit of vanity and egotism.

32. The habit of trying to find shortcuts to success instead of following the marked path of established principles.

33. The habit of contempt for religion, due mainly to a lack of understanding of essential religious principles or over desire for material things.

34. The habit of disloyalty to associates, especially those with whom one works.

35. The habit of refusing to observe and adapt one's self to natural laws.

36. The habit of neglecting to discharge the duties of citizenship by the failure to vote.

37. The habit of meddlesome curiosity; spending time in other people's affairs that could be used to better advantage in the solution of one's own personal problems.

38. The habit of establishing self-limitations because of lack of self-reliance.

39. The habit of allowing others to do one's thinking.

40. The habit of helping to destroy the American way of life by mistaking liberty and freedom as a license instead of a privilege to be safeguarded.

I do not claim that this is the entire catalog of human weaknesses which destroy the power of Organized Individual Endeavor in the average man's life, but it represents the more common weaknesses.

At this point there are two things one may do. First, one may say, "Oh yes, these are the common faults of some people; but they do not apply to me," and pass on. Or, one may say, "I am going to check myself carefully by this list and determine definitely how many of these weaknesses are standing in my way."

Every reader will have to decide for himself which of these

attitudes he will assume. *The decision will be important no matter which way one decides.* The right decision may mark the most important turning point in the life of each reader.

I come, now, to the analysis of ways and means by which an individual may acquire the habit of Organized Individual Endeavor. At the outset let me emphasize the fact that one's success or failure is the result of habits. Observe that the word "habit" preceded each of the forty human weaknesses here described.

Mr. Carnegie has described the thirty-one qualities of leadership, all of which are essentials of the principle of Organized Individual Endeavor. I have presented a brief description of the forty habits which most often stand in the way of application of Organized Individual Endeavor. The first thing one must do, in mastering this principle, is to develop the habit of using the thirty-one qualities of leadership. This habit will tend to eliminate the forty objectionable habits.

Summarized in the briefest manner possible, the following are the steps one must follow in the development of the habit of Organized Individual Endeavor:

1. Adopt a Definite Major Purpose and create a plan for the attainment of that purpose.
2. Form a Master Mind alliance with one or more suitable people, for the attainment of one's Definite Major Purpose, and proceed at once to attain the object of that purpose. Continuous action is essential.
3. Develop the habit of Going the Extra Mile and apply that habit as a means of gaining friendly cooperation in the attainment of one's Definite Major Purpose.

All successful men apply the habit of Organized Individual Endeavor, although sometimes this habit is applied unconsciously. Most failures drift aimlessly, without plan or purpose, their efforts being dissipated because of the lack of Organized Individual Endeavor.

Let us name a few of the outstanding examples of men who moved with Definiteness of Purpose, based upon the principle of Organized Individual Endeavor:

1. Christ, in moral precept and spiritual inspiration.
2. Columbus, in exploration and navigation.
3. Edison, in uncovering and harnessing natural laws, in the field of invention and science.
4. Marconi, in science and invention, in the field of wireless communication.
5. Ford, in self-propelled vehicular transportation.
6. Mahatma Gandhi, in fighting ignorance and superstition among his people.
7. Napoleon, in military operations.
8. Newton, in the study of natural law.
9. The Wright brothers, in aviation.
10. Lincoln, in preserving the unity of the United States.
11. Burbank, in botany and natural law.
12. Marshall Field, in modern merchandising.
13. James J. Hill, in railroading.
14. Andrew Carnegie, in industry and education.
15. John D. Rockefeller, in industry and philanthropy.
16. Louis Pasteur, in fighting disease.
17. George Washington, in military operations and statesmanship.
18. Thomas Jefferson, in statesmanship and founding sound government.
19. Benjamin Franklin, in statesmanship, business, philosophy, and science.

20. Thomas Paine, in philosophy and literature. (He is believed to have done more to start the American Revolution than any other person.)

21. Samuel Gompers, in organized labor.

22. Charles M. Schwab, in the steel industry.

23. Lee de Forest, in science and invention. (He was largely responsible for perfecting the modern radio.)

24. Alexander Graham Bell, in science and invention. (He invented the modern telephone. In his experiments he laid the foundation for radio, by revealing the fact that light waves could be made to pick up and carry the waves of sound.)

25. Edgar Bergen and Charlie McCarthy, in the field of entertainment and ventriloquism, thus offering convincing proof that under the American way of life, where one may act on his own initiative, a man of ordinary ability, and a chunk of wood, can, through Organized Individual Endeavor, bring entertainment to millions of people. In some ways the last illustration is the most important of all I have mentioned. It provides hope and courage to those who have tried and failed many times, as did Edgar Bergen before he "arrived."

In these examples one may find evidence that Organized Individual Endeavor is the master of defeatism. Add to the list the successful men of America whom we have not mentioned, and you will have a catalog of those who have created the American way of life which gives opportunity to each of us who will take the time to organize our efforts and direct them to some definite end.

I come, now, to the detailed description of the method by which one man applied the principle of Organized Individual Endeavor in a manner that yielded more than one million dollars in visible assets, to say nothing of bringing other advantages in the way of opportunities to extend his influence in many directions.

In relating this story I have omitted names of the principals and the mention of the location where the circumstances occurred, because it is one of the characteristics of some men that they do not wish the details of their humble beginnings to be mentioned in the hour of their triumph.

The story began more than *twenty-five years ago*, when a young man visited his wife's people for the first time, shortly after he was married. The last lap of the trip had to be made over an interurban electric railroad which missed the town where his wife's people lived, by two miles. When the train arrived at the country station, from which passengers were usually transported to the town by a horse-drawn hack, no hack was on hand and the two-mile trip had to be made by the young man and his wife on foot.

The incident was exasperating, but it was destined to bring results of a far-flung nature, as we shall soon see. How strange it is that some of the great turning points of a man's life appear at unexpected times, through just such seemingly prosaic circumstances as that which I am about to describe.

When the young man arrived at his wife's hometown, the first of her people to whom he was introduced were her two brothers. They had never seen him before. Therefore it was natural that anything he said at the first meeting would have much to do with the spirit in which he would be received.

Without waiting to lead up to the subject tactfully, this young man lashed out at his brothers-in-law with a question that brought immediate response in the form of a challenge which placed him squarely "on the spot."

"Why," he queried, "don't you have the interurban railroad

company build a spur line into town, so people can ride instead of walking two miles?"

"Well," replied one of the brothers-in-law, "we have been trying to do that very thing for the past ten years, but so far we have been unsuccessful."

"What!" the newly arrived in-law exclaimed. "You have been trying for ten years to do something I could do in three months?"

"Very good," said the brother-in-law. "You have yourself a job before you have been here five minutes."

From this point on, observe carefully and you may see how Organized Individual Endeavor works, even when it is applied by a man who is forced to resort to it because he had talked out of turn. It is one of the tragedies of modern civilization that altogether too often the men who apply the rules of successful achievement stumble upon them by some such incident as this, as the result of necessity, when their backs are to the wall.

"All right," the young man exclaimed, "I'll just take the job and show you that it doesn't require ten years to build two miles of railroad track."

Then he began to get down to business, in real earnestness. In fact, he had placed himself in a position where he had to accept the challenge that had been hurled at him or lose face with his wife's relatives.

By a few questions he learned that the fly in the ointment which had kept the town from being served by the electric railroad was the fact that the road would have to cross a large river, requiring the building of a bridge at a cost of a hundred thousand dollars, that sum being more than the railroad company would agree to invest in the project.

Accompanied by his two brothers-in-law, the young man walked over to the river, to look the situation over, and as they stood there in silence, this is what they saw:

The county road led down a steep riverbank by a winding route, and crossed the river on an old wooden bridge. On the opposite side of the river were about a dozen railroad tracks which formed the storage and switching yard of a steam railroad used to haul coal from that section. After the three men had been standing there for about ten minutes, a train pulled into the yard and blocked the county road. Very shortly a farmer driving a team of horses came up from the far side of the yard and stopped to wait for the crossing to be cleared. In a few minutes another driver came up from the near side and stopped to await the clearing of the crossing.

This was the opening for which the young man was looking. In it he saw the solution of the bridge problem. It is doubtful that he would have seen, in this common, everyday occurrence, anything that his brothers-in-law didn't see if he had not been looking for a way out of the position he had placed himself in by his having talked out of turn.

Fifteen minutes passed and nothing happened. The railroad crossing remained blocked; the teamsters waited! The wheels of the young man's imagination began to turn. In the picture before him he saw the way out of his predicament. How strange it is that the imagination works much better when one is faced by some emergency which calls for action.

Turning to his relatives, the young man exclaimed, "Look! Do you see what I see down there?"

The relatives looked. Yes, they saw a railroad crossing blocked by a train. "But," one of them explained, "that is nothing! I have waited at that same crossing for more than half an hour, many a time. Why, those farmers have been there only ten or fifteen minutes."

"No," the young man muttered to himself in a low tone, "you don't see what I see. I thought not, but I wanted to be sure.

"Well," he continued, "down there is the solution of your bridge problem. Let's break the problem into three parts and solve it one part at a time. The railroad company will pay for a third of the cost of the bridge to get that county road off their tracks, and it will be cheap at that, for someday an accident will occur there that will cost them much more. The county will pay for a third of the cost of the bridge in order to get the county road off those tracks, so people may cross safely. The electric railroad company will pay for a third of the cost in order to extend its road into the town and thereby add a new source of revenue. Your problem is as good as solved, gentlemen!"

The two relatives looked at each other, then they looked at the young man standing beside them. Then, as if they had rehearsed their speech, they exclaimed simultaneously, "Well, I'll be darned! Why haven't we thought of that before?" The two men knew, instantly, that the young man was right. Together the three men spent the following week interviewing the management of the steam railroad company and the electric railroad company and the county commissioners, with the newcomer taking the lead and doing the talking. By the end of the week they had three signatures on a contract, and within three months a spur line of the electric railroad was running into the town.

But this is not the end of the story. It is barely the beginning. The improved transportation facilities provided by the building of the railroad brought new residents to the town and gave the old residents new enthusiasm. The town began to take on new life in a dozen different ways. Among other advantages resulting from the "boom" was one that was very profitable to the relatives of the young man's wife. They owned most of the land adjacent to the town, so they cut it up into building lots and sold it off at a good price. This brought a new building program and provided additional employment.

Having experienced the thrill of local approval in connection with the procuring of the railroad, the young man took on a new lease on life and decided to make the most of his initial success. His brothers-in-law were engaged in producing natural gas, most of which was sold locally. He induced them to increase their operations and extend their service to nearby towns.

Even this did not come anywhere near consuming the supply of gas they had available, so, starting the wheels of his imagination to work again, the young man induced the citizens of the town to form a corporation and enter the business of making glassware, having learned that the glass business required large quantities of fuel. This enterprise not only brought some six hundred new workers to the town, all of whom had to be housed and fed, but the new plant became a customer for the natural gas his relatives had for sale, to the extent of more than three thousand dollars per month.

By this time the newspapers had picked up the story and spread it over their front pages. The young man was nicknamed the "Andrew Carnegie" of the town. The railroad company was so impressed by his initiative that he was retained by the company as assistant to its chief counsel, at a substantial salary.

About a year later his fame had spread until he came to the attention of a large publisher of educational books, and he was employed as the advertising manager, at a salary far greater than men of his age usually receive. He left the town he had helped to sudden prosperity, and later went into business with the publisher. Today his influence touches every village, town, and city in the United States.

Meanwhile, the new enterprises he helped to organize in his wife's hometown extended themselves into sizable operations from which his brothers-in-law became millionaires. The natural gas business became so prosperous that its owners felt obliged to show their appreciation for the work the young man did when the business was young, and they did so by paying the expenses of his three sons through college. Today his eldest son is the head of the business, and well on the road to becoming a millionaire in his own right. His other two sons have responsible positions with the company. The prosperity that came to the merchants and tradesmen of the town as the result of this young man's application of the principle of Organized Individual Endeavor would involve too much detail to justify its description, but it was substantial.

Thus we see how the principle of Organized Individual Endeavor works when it is intelligently and persistently applied.

Analyze this experience as you will; weigh it from any angle you choose; study it step by step and you will be forced to the conclusion that there is nothing about it which could not have been handled by any person of average intelligence and ability.

The success was the result of definite principles persistently applied, and not the result of genius or extraordinary ability.

The success was due to the application of a combination of ten of the principles of individual achievement expressed by Mr. Carnegie.

1. Definiteness of Purpose, carried out through a definite plan that was backed with persistence.

2. The Master Mind actively applied.

3. Applied Faith expressed in terms of persistent action. Passive Faith is powerless.

4. Organized thinking, carried out through definite plans.

5. Creative vision, in the creation of the purpose and the plans for its achievement.

6. Controlled attention, through concentration on the major purpose until it had been achieved.

7. Inspiration, expressed in the enthusiasm with which the job was undertaken and carried through to a finish.

8. Self-discipline, expressed by the temporary change in the young man's personal plans while he was helping his relatives.

9. The habit of Going the Extra Mile, expressed by doing
   that for which he was promised no compensation.

10. Organized Individual Endeavor, expressed by planning
    every move and directing a Definite Major Purpose to its
    logical conclusion.

Too often we see successful men in the hour of their triumph and attribute their success to some form of genius, or to luck, never taking the time to dig deeply into their records to learn how they came by their good fortune.

Take the case of Andrew Carnegie, for example. Those who knew Mr. Carnegie know that his success was due entirely to the application of the principles described in this philosophy, and not to any degree of genius he possessed—unless we may say that genius is the result of painstaking care and persistence in following definite principles. If Mr. Carnegie's career were analyzed step by step it would disclose nothing any more dramatic than, or different from, the experience of the young husband.

The same test would apply to the achievements of Henry Ford and Thomas A. Edison and all the other great Americans who have made this the world's greatest nation. These men, and all others who succeed, do so by knowing precisely what they want and following definite rules in attaining it. If there is one truth which I wish to emphasize above all others in presenting this philosophy, it is the fact that success under the American way of life is attainable by any man of average intelligence who will take the time to familiarize himself with the rules of success and apply them with persistence.

Second in importance to this truth is one I would also like to emphasize, and it is the fact that success is found wherever there is an individual who will master these rules and apply them. The little town mentioned in our story of the young man was about the last place on earth he would have chosen, if he had been deliberately looking for a suitable place for a successful career. Yet by the application of infallible rules of achievement he converted that little town into a veritable gold mine.

Elbert Hubbard did the same thing at East Aurora, New York. When he established himself there nearly half a century ago, the town was not different in any way from a thousand other small towns throughout America. Yet the activities of Mr. Hubbard, carried out through the principles described in this chapter, made East Aurora a Mecca for the whole of this nation, to say nothing of making him richer than he needed to be.

One thing which these and all other successful men have in common is a strict adherence to the principle of Organized Individual Endeavor. Without the aid of this principle a man may struggle for an entire lifetime without gaining more than a bare living, and some fail to do even this well.

Many of us can never hope to be Andrew Carnegies, Thomas Edisons, or Elbert Hubbards; but every American of even average ability can achieve distinction in some line if he will apply the philosophy of achievement with good sense. By way of contrast with more eminent men, consider, for example, the case of a very humble plumber who still lives in the county seat of one of the thirteen original states.

A PLUMBER'S USE OF
THE PRINCIPLES OF ACHIEVEMENT

In a Southern county seat of about ten thousand people there is a very plain man who has made a considerable success of his plumbing business. Since this man has less than average ability in many respects, it is interesting to observe how he has achieved noteworthy success in building up a substantial business which makes him a man of more than ordinary means and influence in his community today.

This man is certainly not possessed of many talents which we ordinarily associate with distinctive achievement. As an employee of a plumbing establishment, he proved to be awkward, clumsy, and not as good as the average pipe fitter. Since he was unsatisfactory in this capacity, his employer tried him out as a salesman and contact man for the business; but in this role he also showed no promise whatever. Although he had no college training, he had finished high school and could write a clear and legible hand. Consequently, his employer thought he might make a satisfactory bookkeeper. Again results were not encouraging. Both employer and employee found the relationship somewhat discouraging in terms of results, but the worker himself began to use his head. Realizing first his definite limitations, he took careful stock of his assets. On the back of an old envelope he listed the following qualities which he knew he possessed:

1. The habit of saving and of handling money carefully.
2. Ability to figure costs on a job with great precision.
3. The ability to recognize superior skill in other men.
4. Persistence in sticking to any task until it is finished.
5. The ability to induce other laborers to work more happily together.

With his envelope before him, this mediocre and somewhat discouraged plumber decided to exercise his own judgment and launch forth a new plumbing business in his own right. Using his own savings, he rented a modest storeroom and announced the new plumbing firm. Almost immediately the best pipe fitter from the old establishment came to him and voluntarily asked to work at whatever wage could be paid in the beginning.

Next the new proprietor looked around and selected a capable salesman and contact man. He promptly found a college boy who was competent in keeping books and handling all correspondence. With good judgment he selected other personnel necessary to supplement his staff for all the business to be done. As business increased, he added other men to his group of employees; but he always chose them very carefully for one or two special skills which they were able to demonstrate effectively.

Having chosen his helpers wisely, he proceeded with his definite purpose of becoming the best and the most prosperous plumber in the county. Before long he had large contracts for several new school buildings and other public projects. He carefully supervised all of the work except the office routine, which he left to his bookkeeper. After a salesman landed a good prospective customer, the proprietor figured all costs and made the bid on the job. In a few years people outside the county were seeking the services of this plumber and his firm because they had established a reputation for high quality of service and of fidelity in full performance of their contracts and trustworthiness in the handling of other people's money and materials.

With a keen eye for economy, the proprietor began to look around for possible expansion of his equipment. Although he was already using a low-rental storeroom for his office and supply room, he decided to invest all of his earnings in the expansion of the business if he could find adequate building space at low cost for the new developments.

About two miles outside of the city he located an old hosiery mill building with a leaking roof and nearly all of the glass windows broken out. This ample two-story building was exactly suited to his needs. Moving cautiously, the ambitious plumber inquired of the owners of the building the rental charges for the whole building. He convinced them that it was better to have a steady income from the property than to leave the building idle.

The owners first asked a relatively high monthly rental on the grounds that it would be necessary for them to do considerable repair work in order to make the building usable. The plumber countered with a suggestion that they quote him the lowest possible rent for the building in its present state and—to his surprise—they actually quoted a figure somewhat less than he was paying for his uptown storeroom. Acting promptly on his own judgment he accepted the offer, took his plumbing staff and repaired the roof of the building, and replaced all of the broken window glasses, thus making substantial improvement in the building that he was about to rent. So pleased were the owners of the building with this fine improvement in the condition of their building that they voluntarily gave the plumber a ten-year lease instead of the one-year lease as agreed for his rental option.

This plumber added to his personnel, increased his stock of supplies, and expanded his services. He achieved a remarkable success during the next few years. In less than ten years he owned the building in which he operated, added a number of skilled workmen who were quite superior to himself in ability in their own lines, and purchased a hundred thousand dollars' worth of supplies. He also found himself invited occasionally to prepare bids for the plumbing work in school buildings, city projects, and other large building ventures in the various counties adjoining his own. All of this business came to him largely through the unchallenged reports about his work by satisfied customers.

There is nothing very unusual about this success story of the plumber except the unusual limitation of his own talents. He was not smart enough to keep his own books, to sell his own services, or to make a good employee in a small city plumbing shop. Employed as a pipe fitter, he was slow, clumsy, and about the worst man on the job, even though he did his best. He had the sound sense, however, to see potentialities in the plumbing business and the opportunity to use his own talents effectively in getting other people to cooperate with him. By concentrating his attention on his definite major aim, he organized all his individual efforts toward achievement of a prosperous and serviceable business which would enjoy the confidence of the people and deserve an adequate financial reward.

This man of modest talents is still operating a thriving business in the old hosiery factory and his reputation is known to contractors, businessmen, and housewives in about five Southern counties. The housewives often comment on the fact that they do not mind paying the plumber when he does a thorough job and the company always has a competent man at work on the assignment in less than half an hour from the time they phone for help.

Most of the facts here related transpired during the treacherous period from the last World War up to the present, and the business has survived all depressions with sound reserves and ever increasing patronage.

Now who says that there are no more opportunities in America for ambitious men? This plumber who had very limited talents, only a high school education, and no funds whatever but the earnings from his own labor, has demonstrated the value of a definite purpose and the value of Organized Individual Endeavor.

If Andrew Carnegie has stressed one point more than all others in his analysis of this philosophy, it is the fact that success is the result of Organized Individual Endeavor. He has emphasized the importance of the Master Mind principle as the chief means of developing personal power through organized effort. He acknowledged that he owed his stupendous achievements to his ability to pick men for his Master Mind group.

While it is true that Organized Individual Endeavor consists of the application of all the other principles of success through proper coordination and the right combination for each circumstance, there is no escape from the fact that the Organized Individual Endeavor principle is the one which assumes the greater importance in connection with all extraordinary undertakings.

As a fitting climax for this chapter, I wish to present an old motto which aptly describes an important point in connection with Organized Individual Endeavor. It is, *"Plan your work, and work your plan."* Nothing can take the place of persistence and continuous application. These are so important that men have been known to succeed through their application alone, without any knowledge of the other principles of success. But be sure that your plan is organized and definite.

AMERICANISM IS A SYSTEM OF HIGHLY ORGANIZED ENDEAVOR

Every person who claims any portion of the bountiful privileges available to the citizens of this country should have a clear picture of the highlights of the American way of life.

Never, in the entire history of the world, has any other nation provided people with as many personal privileges as we of the United States enjoy.

These privileges were purchased with the blood of our forefathers. They have been protected for us with the blood of our own through wars that were waged solely to protect the principle of Organized Individual Endeavor through which we maintain the right of our personal privileges.

The people of the United States have the privilege of moving on their own personal initiative because of a form of government which represents the last word in Organized Individual Endeavor.

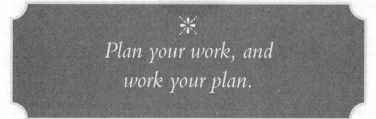

Plan your work, and work your plan.

The leaders of American industry understand the value of the principles demonstrated in this book by such men as Andrew Carnegie, Thomas A. Edison, and Henry Ford. It was by the application of these principles that they attained their leadership, and it reflects enduring credit to their spirit of fairness and their soundness of judgment to know that they encouraged their associate workers in acquiring a working knowledge of this philosophy.

Thus, we live in a country which is geared from stem to stern with an economic system that encourages its people to promote themselves into the highest stations in life that their personal skill and education and experience merit.

I doubt that there could be found in the entire system of American industry a single leader worthy of the privilege of leadership who would not and does not go out of his way to encourage his associate workers to maintain and exercise to the fullest his privilege of personal initiative. The system has been arranged to provide every conceivable form of reward for the encouragement of personal initiative. From these well-known facts we may safely assume that the leaders of American industry believe in giving to every worker, no matter what may be his job, both the privilege and the incentive to develop and use his personal initiative. They believe in it because they know that American industry owes its enviable position to the American way of life through which every citizen is encouraged to promote himself through his own initiative.

The time is at hand when the people of this country need to appropriate Andrew Carnegie's gift and put it to work. The time is appropriate because the American way of life is being destroyed from within our own borders. The major attack is against American industry which, incidentally, is the very jugular vein of the American economic system.

The American people are at war, whether they recognize this fact or not. Their enemy is resorting to tactics made popular by Adolf Hitler. The substance of such tactics is to "divide and control" the people of America.

In unity there is strength! The time is at hand when the people must recognize this fact and *do something about it or perish*. What can they do?

America is now engaged in a great national defense program. The major need in connection with this program is cooperation and personal initiative among those who are engaged in any branch of American industry. The life of our country depends upon such cooperation. Here, then, is an opportunity for the reader of this book to promote his own interests and at the same time make his contribution to the program through which the right of personal initiative is being protected for the people of America as a whole.

The present emergency calls upon every person to make some sort of contribution for the preservation of the American way of life. What greater service could any man render, at this time, than that of helping to fight the enemy which seeks to "control and divide" the people?

The philosophy of success set forth in this book is perfectly suited for this purpose. It not only helps to protect Americanism, but it is Americanism in a highly organized form. Moreover, it is presented in a form which enables the individual to appropriate and use it for his individual benefit. At the same time he is able to use it as a means of wiping out the subtle forces of destruction which are "dividing and controlling" the people of America. In this way, we can master the subtle enemy with which Adolf Hitler threatened to "mop up America from within." *Let us fight fire with a stronger fire!* Thus we may not only promote the individual interests of the American people, but also help save the soul of the American way of life.

At the present pace at which this country is piling up indebtedness for the coming generations, the youth of America will need every possible form of knowledge and a complete mental discipline with which to meet this emergency. Moreover, no one knows at the present where our national debt will end, but this much we do know: The people of America, both this and the generations which follow ours, will need a sound philosophy through which to increase their earning power. Income taxes and other forms of taxation have already become a heavy burden for many, although apparently the present tax burden is mild when compared with that which seems inevitable for the future.

Even though we manage to save the American way of life from total destruction, we will nevertheless be confronted still with a heavy tax burden that will deprive the people of the freedom of mind and the liberty they have known in the past. *From this conclusion there is no escape!*

Let us face these facts and prepare to meet them—not by restricting free enterprise and personal initiative by law, but by teaching the people how to add to their income by the fullest possible exercise of their personal initiative.

To this end, I offer my contribution through the philosophy which has served as the foundation of every success this country has known. This philosophy offers our own and future generations a practical means of meeting the heavy tax burdens that are sure to overtake us with an increase of our incomes.

It is neither likely nor probable that we shall wish to meet the heavy taxation of the future by discarding our automobiles, radios, and modern conveniences of life. Nor is it proper that we should do so. America still is the richest and the greatest nation of the world, but our riches will not begin to meet our tax bills, let alone maintain our present standard of living, unless we stop the present trend toward a desire for something for nothing and find new and better ways of rendering useful service.

As Andrew Carnegie has so well stated, the riches of America consist of a combination of our natural resources and the education, experience, and skill of the leaders who have developed these resources. The only difference between this country as we know it today, and the time when it was discovered, is that which has been added to it through the *personal initiative* of the men who have developed our American industry and helped to build the foundation stones of Americanism.

Riches, in their highest form, consist of useful service! Let those of us who seek personal riches remember this truth. Let those who pass laws restricting personal initiative also remember that such laws destroy the major source of all riches.

What the people of America need now, and in the future, is encouragement in the exercise of their rights to free enterprise and personal initiative—not a penalty on these privileges.

A prophet foretells the future by looking into the past! We need not be seers to look back over the past few years and see, as clearly as we can see the sun on a cloudless day, that we have been drawn into a whirlpool of forces which have already gone far toward the destruction of the American way of life entirely.

One by one the foundation stones of Americanism have been undermined, until not one of them is standing on solid ground today. We know how these foundation stones are being destroyed. We know who our enemies are. We have uncovered the technique with which the American way of life is being rapidly destroyed. And we know, beyond all possible doubt, that nothing but *Organized Individual Endeavor* can save us from the loss of much that we, as Americans, cherish.

The particular form of Organized Individual Endeavor that we need now is the organization of his majesty the king, known as *Public Opinion*. When the sovereign will of the people speaks, the whole world stops, looks, and listens! This sovereign is still the master in the United States, *but even kings lose their power when they neglect to use it.* Right now our sovereign needs a new awakening! He has gone to sleep on his job. Meanwhile, the enemies of the sovereign are active. They are gnawing away at the king's throne. Applying the foreign-born principle of "dividing and controlling," these enemies have centered their attention upon the major foundation stone of Americanism (the American form of government), and they are dividing it against itself.

So the time is at hand when the people of the United States must decide, and decide now, whether or not they wish to give up their right to the exercise of *personal initiative*. Upon that decision will depend the future of Americanism.

We must act. We must "plan our work, and work our plan" through the exercise of Organized Individual Endeavor as detailed in this chapter.

YOU HAVE IMPORTANT WORK TO DO TODAY.

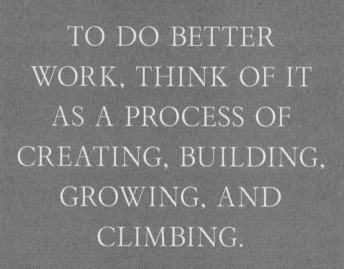

TO DO BETTER
WORK, THINK OF IT
AS A PROCESS OF
CREATING, BUILDING,
GROWING, AND
CLIMBING.

NOTHING CAN
TAKE THE
PLACE OF WORK
EXCEPT FAILURE.

ABOUT THE AUTHOR

Napoleon Hill was born in 1883 in Wise County, Virginia. He worked as a secretary, a "mountain reporter" for a local newspaper, and the manager of a coal mine and a lumberyard, and attended law school, before he began working as a journalist for *Bob Taylor's Magazine*—a job that led to his meeting steel magnate Andrew Carnegie, which changed the course of his life. Carnegie urged Hill to interview the greatest industrialists, inventors, and statesmen of the era in order to discover the principles that led them to success. Hill took on the challenge, which lasted twenty years and formed the building block first for *The Law of Success* (also published by TarcherPerigee), and later for *Think and Grow Rich*, the wealth-building classic and all-time best seller of its kind. After a long and varied career as an author, magazine publisher, lecturer, and consultant to business leaders, the motivational pioneer died in 1970 in South Carolina.